Creating a Computer-Supported Writing Facility: A Blueprint For Action

Advances in Computers and Composition Studies

Series Editors:

Gail E. Hawisher
Purdue University

Cynthia L. Selfe
Michigan Technological University

Creating a Computer-Supported Writing Facility: A Blueprint for Action

Cynthia L. Selfe
Michigan Technological University

Foreword

Arthur P. Young
Clemson University

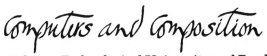

Michigan Technological University and Purdue University

Published by *Computers and Composition*, Michigan
Technological University, Houghton, Michigan 49931 and
Purdue University, West Lafayette, Indiana 47907.

Library of Congress Cataloging-in-Publication Data

Selfe, Cynthia L.
Creating a computer-supported writing facility:
A blueprint for action.

Includes index.

89-92011
ISBN 0-9623392-0-2

Book design by James R. Kalmbach, Illinois State
University. Cover design by Katherine Knight, Michigan
Technological University.

To Bunky Buns and Houghton, America.
Amazing Grace

Series Design Editor:

James R. Kalmbach
Illlinois State University

Volume Assistant Editor:

C. Randall Chafy
Michigan Technological University

Volume Copy Editors:

Leslie M. Bowen
James R. Cichoracki
Lisa A. Eary
Jack P. Hursh
Pamela Moravec
Kent J. Polkinghorne
Amy J. Sullivan
Timothy R. Zuellig
—Michigan Technological University

Table of Contents

Section One: Planning for a Computer-Supported Writing Facility

Section Two: Operating a Computer-Supported Writing Facility

Section Three: Improving a Computer-Supported Writing Facility

List of Figures

Foreword

This book is not only a superb introduction to creating, administering, and improving computer-supported writing facilities, it is a wonderful blueprint for action that goes beyond computers and writing instruction to demonstrate ways to build consensus and collegiality among faculty in support of teaching, research, program development, and other educational goals. Cindy Selfe's purpose is to provide a thoughtful process for establishing and maintaining a computer-supported writing facility that is conceived and administered as an important representation of a faculty's teaching philosophy and practices. Thus, this book does not begin with recommendations on which computer systems to buy or which software packages to use, but rather, it begins with strategies for assisting faculty in identifying their most important assumptions about writing, writers, and writing instruction. After faculty articulate these assumptions to each other within the department and to others without the department, including administrators and computer specialists, they are then ready to plan and to develop a computer facility based on what they know about composition theory and pedagogy and not what someone else knows about computer hardware and software.

This collaborative planning process often produces for participating faculty a sense of commitment to this new and important concept for improving students' writing abilities. Without such faculty commitment, computer facilities remain on the fringe of the central business of English departments—instruction in writing, reading, and literature. Facilities developed without general faculty consensus and commitment often become peripheral activities, important only to the few faculty responsible for the facilities' administration. This book is a guide to avoiding this prevalent pitfall in academic decision-making, and it is a guide to developing a community in which writers and the teaching of writing are nurtured, valued, and enhanced.

As the author of this book, Cindy Selfe has included much practical advice based on her experiences as the founder and director of the Center for Computer-Assisted Language Instruction (CCLI) at Michigan Technological University and as a consultant to numerous colleges and universities across the country. Readers will find step-by-step procedures for training students and teachers to use the facility. In addition, readers will appreciate specific examples of recordkeeping forms for collecting data useful in documenting the facility's current use, for evaluating the facility's effectiveness, and for planning the facility of the future. However, the hidden benefits that accrue when teachers work together as a "community of scholars" to articulate their assumptions about writing and learning and to make important decisions about the facilities which will support their teaching may be this book's most important message. Such benefits are: new opportunites for faculty in teaching, research, and program development; collaborative projects among teachers and between teachers and students; a renewed commitment to teaching; and a heightened awareness of the importance of collegiality in departmental activities.

On a more personal note, I was pleased that the Editors of the *Advances in Computers and Composition Studies* asked me to write a Foreword to this particular volume, *Creating a Computer-Supported Writing Facility*, which focuses on developing writing programs and creating the facilities to support them. From 1976 until 1987, I served as Head of the Department of Humanities at Michigan Technological University. During those years, an incredibly knowledgeable, collegial, and resourceful faculty developed several writing programs: a nationally recognized writing-across-the-curriculum program, undergraduate and graduate degree programs in scientific and technical communication, a reading/writing tutorial center, the Institute for Research on Language and Learning, and the CCLI. This latter facility was planned to be consistent with the faculty consensus and philosophy of composition which enabled the other programs to be successful, and it created an opportunity for faculty to review their assumptions about the teaching of writing and to renew their commitment to these departmental programs.

Certainly, in the development of the CCLI there were many administrative hassles along the way. There were disagreements over what the budget allocation should be and who should control it, disagreements over whether the CCLI should be a university facility or a departmental facility—and what administrative and bureacratic decisions would follow as a result. But now that the CCLI is a reality and serving student majors and nonmajors alike, serving writing teachers as well as other teachers across the curriculum who offer "computer-intensive courses," the adminstrative headaches seem minor and temporary, a necessary condition, as it were, to a program that is healthy and growing and thereby producing the anxiety and tension that necessarily accompanies changes.

What I remember most about the seventeen years I spent at Michigan Tech was not the inevitable bureacratic hassles associated with developing innovative academic programs, but rather the talented and collegial faculty that could plan programs and then implement them, the friendly and bright students who built better bridges between the humanities and technology than most of their instructors, and the supportive administration that provided the necessary resources for quality instruction—from the hardware and software for the CCLI to an entirely renovated building for the arts and humanities. I remember, too, the energetic and imaginative leadership that Cindy Selfe brought to the development of our computer-supported writing facility, a leadership that was absolutely vital to establishing a successful facility central to the most important teaching and scholarly aspirations of the department. This book reveals the role that knowledge and good sense plays in teaching writers, administering writing programs, and developing computer-supported writing facilities.

Arthur P. Young
Clemson University
Clemson, South Carolina
August 1989

Preface

Creating a Computer-Supported Writing Facility: A Blueprint for Action is the inaugural volume in the series *Advances in Computers and Composition Studies*. The series seeks to provide a set of volumes that focus on the issues associated with the use of computers in writing and writing instruction, with particular emphasis on today's problems and tomorrow's possibilities for learning in the Electronic Age. An assumption underlying the series is that the computer is a powerful tool already transforming the ways in which we write, read, learn, teach, and think.

In the late twentieth century, we are witnessing a profound change in the technology of literacy, a change that affects not only the activities of reading and writing but also of learning and teaching literacy. The technological changes from stylus and clay tablet through ink and paper to movable type and now to electronic media have implications for writing and teaching writing that have only begun to manifest themselves. *Advances in Computers and Composition Studies* seeks to explore many of these implications through a careful selection of volumes that address issues of technological change.

One of the settings that has been radically altered by technology is the writing lab, and this particular volume suggests procedures for establishing a computer-supported writing lab that are congruent with humanistic concerns. Cynthia Selfe argues that computer writing centers must not be driven by the technology which they house but rather by the needs of English departments—their students, their faculty, and their programs. To this end, Selfe suggests a series of procedures that should be grounded in current writing theory, research, and pedagogy. Her emphasis is on creating a setting for writers that uses technology to facilitate collaboration and conversation, research and learning, planning and composing. It should be a setting that attracts students and faculty rather than an environment that is sterile and forbidding. By following Selfe's procedures, individual English departments can tailor their labs to suit their own particular requirements and goals.

This book grows out of the author's considerable experience in directing the computer-supported writing facility at Michigan Tech and in her continuing work with high schools and universities from throughout the country. Many of the problems highlighted in this selection Selfe learned of firsthand from her yearly summer workshops for writing teachers. Such a book addresses the problems teachers encounter as they attempt to integrate technology into English programs. I know of no other individual more qualified to address the issues encapsulated in this volume than Cynthia Selfe. Her knowledge and experience as presented in this volume become, I believe, reference points for anyone wanting to design a technological space for writers and their texts.

Gail E. Hawisher
Purdue University
West Lafayette, Indiana
August 1989

Introduction

It is 1989. The last real battles of the computer revolution in English composition classrooms at the college level are all but over, and our work as a profession has just begun. The most reluctant among us now accept that there is some role for computers in the teaching of written language, but not even the most enthusiastic claim to know just what that role should be. Indeed, if our current use of computers is marked by any common theme at all, it is experimentation at the most basic level. As a profession, we are still grappling with computers, struggling to find new perspectives from which we can assess the roles of computers in English/language arts and the teaching of writing.

Nowhere is there greater potential for achieving a degree of success in this difficult venture than in the numerous computer-supported writing labs/classrooms that have recently been set up in colleges and universities across the country. These facilities, often small rooms containing four or five microcomputers, are commonly nourished within the protective environment of a traditional reading/writing center and are supported by the administrative structure of an existing English, language arts, or composition program. Because these labs/classrooms often enjoy broad-based departmental support and a focus on language activities, they can become places where teachers and students gain the experience necessary to use technology in an unconventional computer environment—one not controlled by the thinking of computer scientists and not constrained by the traditional mathematics-oriented uses of the computer's power.

Computer-supported writing labs/classrooms, however, are not guaranteed to provide the professional "elbow room" necessary for constructing our profession's new vision of computers and their role in writing programs. Their success depends on inventive faculty who take a unique, language-oriented approach to the design and operation of a computer facility, and the instructional activities conducted therein.

This book is designed for English composition teachers in college or university settings who want to (or are asked to) establish and maintain a computer-supported writing lab/classroom. The three main sections of the text focus on planning, operating, and improving such facilities and are informed directly by the three fundamental suggestions that follow:

SUGGESTION #1: Plan computer-supported writing labs/classrooms so that they are tailored to writers, writing teachers, and writing programs, not computers.

SUGGESTION #2: Ground daily lab/classroom operations and instruction in the best of current writing theory, research, and pedagogy.

SUGGESTION #3: Improve labs/classrooms by focusing on the writing programs and the writers' communities they support.

The assumptions underlying these suggestions are simple: to build a successful computer-supported writing center, to sustain operations, and eventually to improve the support such a facility provides, English composition teachers need to start with what they know about writing and teaching rather than what they know about technology. They should focus on research and theory in rhetoric, linguistics, and reading rather than on machines. Building on this firm foundation, English teachers can then use computers in innovative, nontraditional, and productive ways.

Section One

Planning for a Computer-Supported Writing Facility

Chapter One

Defining Computer-Supported Writing Facilities

Perhaps the only thing computer-supported writing labs and classrooms currently share is variety. The goals of these facilities reflect the richness and diversity of our profession: some exist to support traditional reading/writing centers; some support entire writing programs; some offer electronic tutorials on grammar and usage, or style editors for revision; and others provide electronic networks for the exchange and critique of drafts in process. Computer-supported writing labs and classrooms may concentrate only on document-design projects involving text and graphics, serve more broadly as classrooms for all language-intensive courses within an English department, or even share space and resources with other disciplines.

And the differences go beyond goals and instructional focus. No single standard, for instance, exists for software and hardware; generally such matters are determined by the needs and preferences of faculty and students who work in the facilities or administer daily lab operations. Successful labs/classrooms may use mainframe, mini-, or microcomputers; offer text-analysis packages, grammar tutorials, or invention software; and maintain one word-processing package or an entire library of such packages.

Budgets and staffing, too, vary as widely as the finances of the writing programs which sponsor these labs or classrooms. Some are funded by English departments; others are funded at the institutional level by an entire school or college. Funding, in turn, affects operational control and expenditures. Some facilities are able to employ consultants knowledgeable about both writing and computer technology; some depend solely on the expertise of users. Some centers remain open twenty-four hours a day, others only a few hours each week.

Nor can labs/classrooms be aptly characterized by size, room decor, number and kind of computers, the configuration of hardware, the technical support they enjoy, their furniture and floor plan, their ambience and networking capabilities. All of these elements vary widely, as do the ways in which staff members of each center handle the controversial issues of user access, teacher and student training, documentation, privacy, plagiarism, and security.

A few broad commonalities for such labs/classrooms do, however, exist. We will identify these shared characteristics to define the term "computer-supported writing facility" as this text uses it. First, the rooms about which we are concerned are set up as walk-in laboratories, classrooms, or combination labs/classrooms to support the business and teaching of writing with computer technology. Most frequently, these centers grow out of existing writing or composition programs. Typically, computer-supported writing facilities have between five and twenty-five microcomputers, maintain a central focus on word processing and document design, and have some connection with an English department or faculty.

Establishing a Successful Computer-Supported Writing Facility

Unfortunately, this generic definition of a computer-supported writing facility provides little guidance for academic institutions that want to establish a successful lab or classroom, one that will support the goals of a particular writing program. Such an effort, in fact, requires much more than attending to guidelines and definitions that have been previously established. Rather, it necessitates the involvement of innovative and creative faculty who are willing to undertake a careful program of planning and design, see that the daily operations of a lab/classroom are well grounded in the best of current writing theory and research, and use the lab resources to encourage and support writers' communities within a particular academic setting.

The next two chapters in this section describe the process of designing a lab/classroom that will support an existing English composition program.

Chapter Two

Building on Existing Writing Progams

One of the best pieces of advice for teachers who accept the charge of establishing a computer-supported writing facility (and, incidentally, the hardest to follow) is to forget about computers and concentrate on writing. This chapter explains why such a tactic is important to the eventual success of a computer-supported writing lab or classroom.

The first half of the chapter outlines the advantages of focusing on writing and the teaching of writing when designing computer-supported facilities and describes the new "vision" of technology that is fostered by such an approach. This section explains why English teachers, even those who are naive about computer technology, can serve as more effective primary designers of innovative computer-supported writing facilities than can the computer specialists who are often hired to take on such tasks.

The second half of the chapter offers some specific advice about how to begin the challenging task of design. It outlines a process of identifying assumptions about writing and the teaching of writing that will ultimately shape the design, operation, and continual improvement of a successful computer-supported writing facility.

Forgetting What We "Know" About Computers

Traditional *computer* labs and computer-supported *writing* facilities are two very different kinds of places. In one, computers come first; in the other, writers do. On this relatively simple statement rests the fundamental success of any computer-supported writing center.

When computer-supported writing labs/classrooms grow out of existing composition programs under English departments, and when they are staffed by faculty with academic training in the study of language, rhetoric, or communication, they can be special places. These facilities, because they have a natural focus on language activities, can become places in which teachers and students formulate an autonomous and creative sense of the computer's role within composition programs while still keeping attention focused on writers and the activity of writing. In these labs/classrooms, we can learn to use technology in an unconventional computer environment— one not constrained by the thinking of computer scientists or the traditional mathematics-oriented uses of the computer's power.

Unfortunately, because our profession has come so recently to the computer revolution, we have not always recognized the primacy of writers and writing in the computer projects we have undertaken. In fact, we have thus far been satisfied to build our professional vision of computers on two relatively limited conceptual foundations—one imported from outside our profession and one imported from the past. These two influences have hindered our attempts to create a "writer-centered" view of computer support.

To understand the importance of formulating this new writer-centered vision of computers, we need to look closely at the current, relatively limited use of computers with which we have contented ourselves as a profession and determine why such limited use has been less than successful.

First, English programs have been content to "see" and "understand" computers in terms of their use in other fields. Relying on such imported visions, individual writing teachers often find themselves operating in environments that cannot support the work of composing in any realistic fashion. An English department may, for example, purchase a roomful of terminals on the recommendation of a colleague in mathematics, hook those terminals up to the campus mainframe, and require teachers to struggle, along with their students, to master the awkward line editor available on this centralized machine. Only after much frustration do the teachers in such programs recognize that most mainframe editors are not designed to accommodate the complexly recursive revisions; the large-scale reorganizations; and the experiments with arrangement, order, and style that mark the composing processes of most writers.

The frustration that these teachers feel is the result of not only choices involving hardware. Operating under a similar vision, English composition programs have bought stand-alone microcomputers and, imitating lab layouts observed in a College of Business, placed them neatly in rows, in study carrels built with high sides and padded with sound-proofing materials. Later, the teachers in these programs discover the critical disadvantages of such an arrangement: that it inhibits the rich collaborative exchanges which take place among writers working on a common assignment, that it discourages the valuable discussions of rhetorical problems which mark the interaction of writers functioning as a peer group, and that it limits the sharing of drafts and texts which characterizes writers engaged in on-site conferences.

Second, our profession has been satisfied to understand computer-supported writing facilities in terms of the traditional language-skills labs we have constructed in the past. Operating under such a vision, an English department often "sees" computers as intelligent teaching machines and super typewriters, and establishes a labful of electronic tutors and typewriters in which individual teachers are expected to function effectively, with minimal restructuring of the traditional instructional environment. These labs are seldom attractive to teachers, who see them as limited, remedial, service-related facilities. Nor are they appealing to students, who use them only when absolutely necessary, dropping by to type written assignments or to work through assigned drill-and-practice tutorials on comma placement or spelling errors.

In a crucial sense, these "computer-centered" labs are only tenuously connected with the work of writing and teaching writing. They are seldom the scene of noisy conversations among working writers; they rarely support teacher-student conferences, expressive writing, journal writing, or research and scholarship on writing; they seldom sustain the work of an entire writing class at one time. Facilities designed in such a theoretical and pedagogical vacuum inevitably fail. In this sense, in the sense that our profession has been satisfied to "see" computers according to these imported visions, we may be guilty of subscribing to a limited view of computer-supported writing facilities—a view circumscribed by the paradigms of other disciplines or by our own past experiences with teaching machines and paper-and-pencil composing. Because our vision is limited by tradition, it may also be incapable of accommodating, and indeed taking advantage of, the larger and more radical changes wrought by the electronic medium we are now using. In fact, by subscribing to them, our profession may, as Coleridge says, have created a "tacit compact" (Coleridge, *Biographia Literaria*, pp. 95-96) not to pass beyond a certain limit in speculating about the potential of computer-supported writing facilities.

Now may be the time to take risks in our thinking; to broaden our vision; to experiment; to use computer-supported facilities to accomplish the important goals we have set for ourselves as writers and teachers of writing.

Remembering What We Know About Writing

Certainly one reason computer-supported writing labs/classrooms have the potential for providing a unique kind of technological vision within composition programs is that such facilities can be shaped by the same set of assumptions about writing and the teaching of writing that inform the English composition programs in which the labs/classrooms exist.

In fact, the process of finding and mapping these rhetorical and pedagogical "roots" can provide the healthiest foundation for making systematic and informed decisions about the design and instructional goals of a computer-supported facility: for making decisions about hardware purchases, machine configurations, software packages, room layout, scheduling, and even machine maintenance. It is this deceptively simple and powerful process of starting with concerns about the English curriculum rather than about computers, of shaping computer use to the teaching of writing (and not vice versa), that allows a lab to grow organically and successfully out of an existing composition program.

Of course, such a process is not a "quick fix." It necessarily involves a large investment of time and professional energy on the part of any English department. Faculty connected with the design of a computer-supported lab/classroom need to spend time identifying three important components of a writing program that will shape the proposed facility:

- Students' writing needs within the composition program;

- The faculty's personal assumptions about writing, gleaned from their experiences as writers;

- The faculty's professional assumptions about how to teach writing, tempered by their experience in the classroom.

Each of these components can and should shape the design and operation of a computer-supported writing facility.

The remaining sections of this chapter discuss the importance of collecting information in each of these areas and suggest how a systematic effort to gather such information might proceed.

Considering Students' Writing Needs

As a profession, we continue to learn how to teach writing more effectively. Our research and scholarship during the last decade indicates the importance of approaching writing as a social activity and as a series of related processes; of identifying audience and purpose in rhetorical situations; of providing both evaluative and personal feedback to writers; and of recognizing the essential connections between writing, reading, listening, and speaking. Rather than bring computers into our classroom as electronic gadgets, we should use computers and computer-supported instruction as tools to teach students these fundamental concepts and do so in a way that complements instruction. Computer-supported instruction, in other words, like any type of writing instruction, should help us address the specific problems that our students exhibit when they compose.

So, the first step for designing an effective computer-supported writing facility involves forgetting about computers and assessing our students' writing needs. Most of our pedagogical practices and theoretical assumptions in the writing classroom grow directly out of the observations we make of student needs. We watch our students, we see how they write and from what writing problems they suffer, and we draw certain conclusions.

With each student we help, these conclusions become stronger, more certain, and we modify our instruction according to the lessons we learn. Thus our interpretations are refined with each successive observation.

In a pattern we try to follow throughout this book, Figure 2.1 shows how one sample faculty might have gone about devising a list of their students' writing needs and problems in a ten-minute workshop or seminar activity, clustering these activities under several main headings, and then identifying a broad instructional priority for each type of problem.

In fact, these responses do not represent the work of any one faculty; rather, they are compiled from the answers of real teachers from a range of educational settings who have responded to these activities in workshop situations. They serve to give readers a general, and yet realistic, sense of how the tasks of designing, planning for, and operating a computer-supported writing facility might proceed in their own institutions.

Figure 2.1: Identifying Students' Writing Needs

What are our students' writing problems and their instructional needs?

Process	**Mechanical**
invention	parallelism
planning	agreement
getting started	attribution
revising in	
multiple drafts	spelling
editing	sexist language

Attitude	**Logic**
commitment to writing	organizing paragraphs
fear/apprehension	organizing essays
understanding	general vs. specific
importance of	topic sentences
writing in career	
development	
refusal to revise	

Do we share a common sense of instructional priorities for addressing these problems?

Different students, at different points in their developmental process, with different problems, and different abilities all make it impossible to assign across-the-board priorities. However, it was generally agreed that we share the following approach to writing problems:

PRIORITY #1: Attitude toward writing
PRIORITY #2: Process-based problems
PRIORITY #3: Product-based (logic) problems
PRIORITY #4: Mechanics and style

You might have noticed that the writing needs identified by the sample faculty are clustered under headings that make these items easier to discuss in terms of instructional priority. The note added to the end of the listing indicates the faculty's feeling about the general priorities of these writing needs.

Teachers' Assumptions About Writing

From their experience in identifying and answering students' writing needs, as well as from their readings in the field of English composition, most teachers of writing have also identified for themselves a set of philosophical premises that inform their instruction. A faculty member might believe, for instance, that writing involves a socially-based problem-solving *process* as well as an end *product*, or that all authors can benefit from feedback as they work through the writing process. Teachers test and modify these premises continually; each student and each writing-intensive class provides data that support the assumptions or that indicate a need for modification.

These same premises serve as the focus of our second step in the design process; if carefully articulated, they can help to inform the establishment of, and indeed the daily operation of, a computer-supported writing facility. In fact, if a faculty can identify and agree on a shared set of assumptions, and then use them to determine the instructional priorities of a computer lab/classroom, the specific goals of that facility will necessarily provide a close match for a department's general instructional effort in composition and assure a cohesive approach to the teaching of writing overall. Similarly, a faculty which fails to identify assumptions about writing before designing a computer-supported writing lab runs the risk of creating a facility that is philosophically unrelated to the rest of their instructional activities.

In Figure 2.2, for example, is a list of assumptions about writing that might have been compiled by our sample faculty as they met together in an afternoon workshop session to think about designing a computer-supported writing facility. You might want to examine the list, and see if you have any theoretical premises in common.

Figure 2.2: Identifying Teachers' Assumptions About Writing

What do our experiences as writers tell us about the task of solving written communication problems?

ASSUMPTION #1: Writing involves a complex process of planning, drafting, revising, and editing activities that occur in dynamically recursive patterns.

ASSUMPTION #2: Writing to learn (expressive writing, journal writing, free writing) is fundamentally different from writing to communicate (transactional writing).

ASSUMPTION #3: The development of writing skills is determined by the developmental process of human learning.

ASSUMPTION #4: Writing, because it involves crystallizing thought into linguistic symbols, necessarily involves learning and thinking.

ASSUMPTION #5: Everyone has a different set of writing problems and writing skills.

ASSUMPTION #6: Different writing purposes (to persuade, to inform, to express, to amuse) and different writing modes (narration, description, classification, etc.) involve different challenges, skills, and activities for students.

ASSUMPTION #7: Writing and reading are more than complementary skills; they are integrally connected at the most basic physical and cognitive levels.

In glancing over this list, you probably noticed that the faculty's assumptions about writing are stated in general terms and follow no particular pattern of rank or logic. In fact, a group of teachers may be asked to take only five or ten minutes for this brainstorming task and to record those assumptions that come immediately to mind when they think about writing.

Teachers' Assumptions About Teaching Writing

The observations teachers make of students' writing problems shape not only their assumptions about the act of writing but also their assumptions about the most effective ways to *teach* writing. These assumptions about teaching writing, in turn, determine the type of instruction that goes on within any writing classroom or program. For example, if a teacher assumes that writing involves a process as well as a final product and observes students having trouble with various parts of that process (invention, for instance, or revising a preliminary draft), then the necessity of teaching students process-oriented strategies for solving writing problems becomes obvious. Similarly, if a teacher believes that all authors can benefit from feedback as they tackle writing problems and notes that students have problems shaping their texts to a reader's needs, the teacher might incorporate instruction in peer-audience feedback into writing classes.

The task of identifying these assumptions about how writing should be taught should also have a direct influence on instruction in a computer-supported writing facility. Hence, we suggest that this task form the basis for our third step in the design process.

In fact, teachers who are familiar with any writing lab or classroom that has failed to win the support of a faculty can attest to the need for this particular activity. Some very real dangers lie in trying to construct a computer-supported facility while ignoring what English composition instructors think about the teaching of writing. Many of these projects have begun with adequate funds and good intentions. One English department, for example, received a $105,000 grant to design and establish a working computer-supported writing facility. The project began with the goal of designing a lab/classroom that would be used by all English instructors in the department's writing program. Unfortunately, in planning the facility and outfitting it with hardware and software, no one took the time to identify the assumptions about teaching writing that the English faculty in this program shared. The following year, to the department's dismay, the computer-supported writing lab remained empty most of the time. English faculty had quickly learned that the lab, which featured a cumbersome word-processing system designed for office use and software tutorials that took a rigid and prescriptive approach to grammar and editing, was of little use to composition classes that emphasized process-based writing instruction.

Although it is an important step in the design process, identifying the precepts an English faculty considers central to the teaching of writing need not be a time-consuming task. In Figure 2.3, we have provided a list of assumptions that our sample faculty might have compiled during a ten- to twenty-minute brainstorming activity in a workshop or seminar setting.

Figure 2.3: Identifying Teachers' Assumptions About Teaching Writing

What are our assumptions about the teaching of writing?

ASSUMPTION #1: Students must practice writing if they are to become better writers.

ASSUMPTION #2: Students must practice writing for different purposes and different audiences, using different modes. Students must be taught strategies for coping with different writing situations.

ASSUMPTION #3: Students must be guided through various processes of writing and be taught specific strategies for use at various points in these processes.

ASSUMPTION #4: Students must receive critical feedback from readers (both peers and teachers) at all stages of their writing processes.

ASSUMPTION #5: Students must learn to read critically their own writing and the writing of others—always with an eye toward revision.

ASSUMPTION #6: Students must be given instructional help and practice in mastering their own unique writing problems in the context of real writing tasks.

ASSUMPTION #7: Students must be given sufficient time to practice writing and rewriting.

ASSUMPTION #8: Students must be given chances to succeed in writing situations, even if this means continued rewriting efforts.

ASSUMPTION #9: Students should also be shown how other writers, both professional and amateur, solve writing problems.

You probably noticed that the pedagogical assumptions the sample faculty listed in this example relate directly to their students' writing problems (Figure 2.1) and their assumptions about teaching writing (Figure 2.2). This consistency makes sense; the faculty's observations of students' writing problems, along with their own experiences as writers, shape their beliefs about writing and about how best to teach writing.

Taking Time for Planning

As you can tell from the previous sections, the combination of activities within this chapter are considerable and will generally require more than one meeting of a faculty. The completion of all three initial design steps might well involve a series of small group discussions among teachers of writing-intensive courses, a program of departmental colloquia, or several meetings of an English faculty.

The time invested in these activities will be well spent. Once a faculty identifies a set of premises and assumptions they can agree on in connection with the teaching of writing, they have the basis for making a consistent set of informed decisions about any large scale curricular change—from the addition of a new sequence of writing courses to the design of a computer-supported writing facility.

Chapter Three

Identifiying Goals and
Making Planning Decisions

In the preceding chapter, we discussed the advantages of "forgetting" about computers and "remembering" about writing—an approach we recommend for teachers beginning the process of designing a computer-supported writing lab/classroom. In the current chapter, we extend this process, explaining how teachers can translate the goals of an existing writing program into a set of concrete instructional and operational goals that drive a computer-supported writing facility. We also demonstrate how a clearly defined set of instructional and operational goals can assist lab/classroom administrators in making

decisions about hardware and software purchases, lab/class-
room layout, staffing, and budgetary concerns.

Identifying The Goals of a Computer-Supported Writing Facility

During the last decade, computers have come to play an increasingly central instructional role in writing-intensive classes
wherever they are taught across the English curriculum.
The advantages of this movement are clearly evident; in
many cases, computers have brought new vigor and perspective to the teaching of writing. Unfortunately, rapid growth
also has concomitant disadvantages. In the rush to buy new
equipment, to purchase new software, to establish a modicum
of computer literacy among faculty members, we have not often
had time as professionals to take care in the planning of
computer use and computer facilities to support English composition programs.

It is not unusual for English faculty to return to school in
September to find themselves involved in the administration of
a new word-processing lab/classroom that has been established
in their absence. Frequently labs/classrooms, even those that
are used primarily for word processing, are outfitted with
hardware and software on the recommendations of computer-
science teachers or business instructors rather than on those of
English composition instructors. The end result of such efforts
are usually computer labs that cannot support, in any realistic
way, the activities of writers.

To avoid these situations, English faculty must take the
initiative in planning for computer labs/classrooms that are
designed for writers by teachers of writing and grow organically out of an existing composition program. The following
sections in this chapter describe briefly how a group of teachers
might go about identifying a set of instructional and operational goals for such computer-supported writing facilities.

Identifying Instructional Goals

In referring to "instructional goals" now and throughout this text, we mean that set of educational objectives that a composition teacher, or teachers, have in mind when presenting material about writers, writing processes, and written texts to students. Individual teachers, of course, construct sets of instructional goals for each lesson, unit, and class that they teach. However, in discussing the instructional goals of a writing program or computer-supported writing facility, we refer specifically to programmatic goals, those objectives shared by a group of teachers that shape a series or collection of writing-intensive classes.

In the best possible cases, an English faculty formulates a set of instructional goals that is both personal and programmatic in nature. Individual members observe students' needs, test current theoretical assumptions about writing against the practice of teaching writing, and compare their conclusions with those of their colleagues. As a larger collective, the faculty meets both formally and informally to articulate a group sense of programmatic instructional objectives.

Making sure that the instructional goals of a computer facility support those of an existing writing program is a relatively straightforward matter once a faculty has identified the assumptions about writing and the teaching of writing that inform their instructional efforts. (See Chapter Two, "Building on an Existing Writing Program.")

After this data about a writing program is gathered, a faculty can use it, in turn, to compile a list of instructional goals for a proposed computer-supported writing facility. These goals will shape all the teaching that goes on in the lab/classroom—whether such instruction involves an entire class of students that uses the computer as a writing aid within the context of a particular course or individual students who use the machines to support their writing in a variety of classes. This planning activity, like most that we suggest, is not, in itself, a lengthy one. In Figure 3.1 is a list of instructional goals for a computer-supported writing center that our sample faculty might have compiled in a fifteen- to twenty-minute workshop session.

Figure 3.1: Instructional Goals of a Computer-Supported Writing Facility

What are the instructional goals that should drive our computer-supported writing facility?

GOAL #1: Encourage students to practice writing as often as possible and to improve their skill as writers.

GOAL #2: Support the concept of writing for a variety of purposes, using different writing strategies, and aiming for different audiences.

GOAL #3: Promote a process-based and reading-intensive approach to writing.

GOAL #4: Encourage collaborative exchanges among writers and teachers of writing: peer feedback, student-teacher conferences, and student-tutor sessions.

GOAL #5: Provide effective, process-based writing instruction for students who request or need it: writing-intensive classes, writing-consultant sessions, and student-teacher conferences.

GOAL #6: Promote critical reading of written texts and instruction in critical reading skills.

GOAL #7: Encourage writers to learn and share successful composing strategies.

As you might have noticed in this list, the sample faculty we have posed were able to translate most of the assumptions they shared about writing and the teaching of writing directly into instructional goals for their computer-supported writing center. This process ensures a lab/classroom that will be as effective as possible in supporting the instructional philosophies and practices of individual faculty members in a particular college or university context.

Establishing Operational Goals

If instructional goals shape the teaching that goes on within a computer-supported writing facility, operational goals shape all other aspects of that facility: staffing of the lab; scheduling of the lab; budgetary concerns; cleaning, maintenance of the lab and the computers within it; layout and arrangement of lab equipment and furniture; access to the lab; purchase and upgrading of software and hardware; and so on.

Ideally, the operational goals of a computer-supported writing facility, the precepts that drive the daily activities within that facility, grow out of the instructional goals that give meaning and purpose to its existence. Such a direct relationship is even more important when a computer facility is designed to support an existing writing program. In Figure 3.2 is a set of operational goals that might have been compiled by our sample faculty.

Figure 3.2: Operational Goals for a Computer-Supported Writing Facility

What are the goals that should shape the daily operations of our computer-supported writing facility?

GOAL #1: Purchase and maintain software and hardware that effectively support a process-based approach to the teaching of writing.

GOAL #2: Provide lab access to any student currently enrolled in a writing-intensive course. Make sure that lab scheduling is flexible enough to accommodate writing communities of any size: individuals, small groups, whole classes, etc.

GOAL #3: Ensure that the lab is administered on a policy level by a teacher(s) of English composition and staffed on a daily basis by consultants who have expertise both in the teaching of writing and in the use of computers as writing tools.

GOAL #4: Ensure that the lab, its layout, its furniture, its decoration, and its ambience provides a comfortable, relaxed writers' environment.

GOAL #5: Provide lab hours that will allow students sufficient time to practice writing and critical reading skills and accommodate individuals' writing habits and processes.

GOAL #6: Provide adequate technical support for maintaining, repairing, and modifying computer hardware/software so that English composition faculty do not have to assume this role.

GOAL #7: Ensure that lab policies encourage process-based writing, collaborative writing activities, and writing as thinking.

GOAL #8: Provide a lab budget administered by an English composition faculty member that is sufficient to support staffing, scheduling, software/hardware purchases, and technical support as described above.

As you can see from this sample, the purpose of such goals is to assure that the daily operations of a computer-supported writing lab/classroom are closely aligned with the instructional goals of that facility. Operational goals give guidance and direction to faculty who must set up the lab's administrative infrastructure once the facility has been created.

Using Instructional and Operational Goals to Plan a Computer-Supported Writing Facility: A Case Study

Once a faculty has identified a set of instructional goals that will inform the educational activities of a computer-supported writing facility and a set of operational goals that shape the daily operations of that facility, other design decisions become increasingly simple to make.

To illustrate this point, I can offer the experience of the Humanities faculty at my home institution, Michigan Technological University, a medium-sized midwestern university that maintains an emphasis on engineering education. Three years ago, when the Humanities faculty at this university began the process of designing a computer-supported writing facility, many of the teachers had already worked together on a seven-year-old writing-across-the-curriculum program. As a result of this experience, many of the teachers on the faculty already shared a set of instructional goals. Although these goals were originally formulated through the experiences of that cross-curricular writing program, they nevertheless provided valuable guidance for the design of the computer facility which was created several years later.

The particular instructional goals that this faculty had formulated were not collected overnight in a concerted effort as we suggest in this text. Rather, they grew gradually out of the teachers' professional readings, the research studies they had done in connection with the writing-across-the-curriculum program, and their experience as writers and writing teachers. The goals were quite general in nature and thus amenable to a number of applications.

The faculty had come to the conclusion, for example, that students needed to practice writing and to write for a variety of audiences and purposes if they hoped to become better writers. They had come to believe that teachers of writing had to deal as much with the strategies of composing and composing processes as they did with written texts. They had come to understand that revision plays a pivotal role in the composing processes of most successful writers and that social context shapes rhetorical decisions.

The faculty had also become convinced that these basic premises about writing and the teaching of writing, although they varied slightly in their articulation from colleague to colleague and from year to year, should generally inform the teaching of writing across the humanities curriculum and specifically guide the efforts to establish a computer-supported writing facility.

Each of these assumptions about writing and the teaching of writing had an identifiable impact on the design of the computer-supported writing facility this faculty designed. Their shared emphasis on revision in composing, for example, meant that they had to design a lab that could support a wide range of process-based writing activities and enhance the revision efforts of a wide range of writers. The space they created, therefore, had to be flexible enough to accommodate whole classes of writers as they revised and intimate enough to attract individual authors or small peer groups who wanted to engage in drafting activities. It had to house computers that writers could use when they needed electronic revision aids and empty work tables that they could use for more traditional cutting-and-pasting sessions with hard-copy text.

The faculty's focus on process-oriented revision also facilitated decisions about computer hardware and software in the new lab/classroom. They decided, for example, to purchase microcomputer software that supported revision activities with easy file retrieval and manipulation and a full-screen editor rather than to fight for time on the school's mainframe computer that gave low priority to time-intensive word-processing tasks. In addition, they decided to purchase a brand of microcomputer that could be networked to provide the capability for on-line, peer-group critiques and revision.

Software purchases for the lab/classroom were similarly directed by the faculty's instructional goals. They bought word-processing packages that supported revision strategies, making sure that such programs allowed block moves for students who frequently reordered large chunks of text; appending and concatenation capabilities for students who preferred to revise files separately before combining them into a final document; and windowing for students who wanted to compare sections of alternative drafts. They also bought network software for authors who wanted to post public drafts of their revisions, and created invisible, protected subdirectories for students who preferred revising in the privacy of their electronic journals. For final revision efforts, they purchased programs that could help with stylistic revision, programs that calculated readability levels, and word-processing packages that checked spelling. In other words, the faculty did everything they could think of to create a writer's environment that used technology to support process-oriented revision efforts.

The emphasis on process-based revision also helped the Michigan Tech faculty make a variety of other design decisions about the furnishing and layout, staffing, and location of the lab/classroom. For example, rather than arranging computers in the rank-and-file rows that marked traditional computer labs in other settings around the university, faculty put the work stations in clusters to facilitate the exchange of revision suggestions and participation in collaborative writing activities. In this way, teachers who held classes in the computer facility were able to encourage the same shouting, arguing, and intellectual dialectic that went on when peer groups operated in traditional classrooms. The faculty also decided to furnish the lab/classroom with discussion tables where students could meet in peer groups to talk about rewriting strategies and set up several tables where students could gather to mark up hardcopy drafts. Using similar assumptions about writing and teaching writing, these teachers decided to staff the lab/classroom with trained composition consultants who could provide feedback on writing strategies as well as on computer strategies and to place the departmental lab/classroom in the same building as the faculty offices so that student-teacher writing conferences would be readily accessible.

Advantages of a Writing-Centered Design Process

The organic, writing-centered design process sketched briefly in this chapter has several advantages. On a broad professional level, it can encourage English composition teachers to create computer-supported facilities predicated on the conceptual frameworks and instructional goals of English composition teachers rather than on the thinking of computer programmers, marketing experts, computer architects, or statisticians— all of whom have their own ideas of how a computer lab should function. On a more local level, within a particular academic community, the process encourages a faculty to design labs that grow directly out of an existing writing program: a lab that is shaped by established writing-intensive courses and one that is informed by the shared pedagogical values of a particular faculty.

Section Two

Operating a Computer-Supported Writing Facility

Chapter Four

Staffing a Computer-Supported Writing Facility

For English faculty trained as language and composition specialists, the job of operating a computer-supported writing lab can involve some hard lessons in humility and flexibility. In most situations, faculty who already juggle the traditional demands associated with teaching—planning and conducting classes, keeping up with research developments, and serving on departmental committees—find they must also face additional demands: serving as hardware technicians, acting as software consultants, scheduling lab hours, training lab staff, and ordering lab supplies. To succeed in such a situation,

writing faculty who administer a departmental lab/classroom
have to make sure that their work with computers is tied
directly to their work in the classroom, that both endeavors
share a strong commitment to writing and the teaching of writing.

The first steps for assuring such a commitment, as we
discussed in Chapters One through Three, are taken in the
planning and design stage. The next step for assuring this
focus involves finding an innovative, knowledgeable staff who
can carry out the lab's instructional and operational policies.
Far from running themselves, computer facilities consume an
extraordinary amount of human labor—always more than an
academic staff suspects when designing a lab/classroom. In
most cases, making sure that a lab/classroom operates smoothly
on a daily basis requires the coordinated effort of at least three
kinds of people: lab administrators, lab consultants, and lab
technicians.

In this chapter, we discuss how each of these people might fit
into the structure of a computer-supported writing facility and
provide some practical suggestions for faculty members who
must assemble and then train such a staff. As discussed in the
following sections, the specific structure and size of a facility's
staff depends on the educational environment in which the lab/
classroom exists and the writing program that it supports.

Administrators of Computer-Supported Writing Facilities

Although most traditional computer labs are run by computer
specialists as a matter of expediency, this course of action often
proves disastrous for a computer-supported writing facility. As
the planning and design activities in Chapters One through
Three indicate, the success of these labs/classrooms depends on
maintaining a clear theoretical and pedagogical focus on writing and the teaching of writing. For this reason more than any
other, computer-supported writing facilities are best administered by English composition faculty who have a strong grasp

of writing research, theory, and pedagogy.

In some schools, finding a faculty member or members willing to take on this role can be a difficult task. Teachers who specialize in the teaching of writing generally commit themselves to a process-based approach in their own classrooms; their instructional time is taken up with assigning and responding to multiple drafts of papers, conferencing frequently with students, and directing lengthy revision efforts. Given such an instructional load, few writing teachers feel the need or the inclination to take on the additional duties associated with the administration of a computer-supported writing facility.

Ironically, it is the writing teacher's familiarity with writing theory and practice that suits him or her for the role of lab/classroom administrator. A faculty member, with a strong commitment to process-based writing instruction, collaborative writing activities, the use of writing as a thinking tool, and rhetorically-based problem solving will carry these values into the lab/classroom and shape daily operations in support of the classroom activities of other writing teachers. Writing teachers and program administrators, unlike computer experts, are also less likely to allow technology to become the focus of a computer-supported writing facility or to allow decisions to be made with machines, rather than humans, in mind.

The duties and involvement of a teacher/administrator will vary according to the specific academic environment in which he or she functions. In most cases, these individuals oversee the lab budget including expenditures for salaries, hardware and software, repair and maintenance; hire, train, and schedule lab/classroom consultants and technicians; schedule hours for walk-in use and/or regular writing classes; and address matters involving facility policy and programmatic support.

The time that administrators spend on such tasks varies with a number of factors: the age of the lab, the commitment and availability of additional lab personnel, level of lab use by students and other faculty, and the commitment of a department and an institution to the concept of a computer-supported writing facility. Because lab/classroom administrators are frequently academic faculty who teach classes as well as oversee the operations of a computer-supported facility, they are often provided with release time for their activities in connection with computers. Such release time becomes even more crucial if faculty members are expected to publish and maintain an active professional profile. Facilities that contain 20 to 30 machines and support 200-400 writers a term can easily occupy an administrator for 10 hours a week.

Consultants in Computer-Supported Writing Facilities

While administrators make sure that the instructional and operational policies of a computer-supported writing facility are congruent with the values of an existing writing program on a long-term basis, consultants make sure that users, both faculty and students, enjoy the benefit of a supportive writers' environment on a daily basis.

Although the duties of consultants vary within specific educational settings, they are generally put in charge of matters involving day-to-day security, assisting faculty and students who want to learn or to use hardware and software, adapting and producing written documentation and instructions, helping composition teachers who use the lab to teach entire classes of writers, duplicating and archiving software and files, routinely maintaining hardware, ordering expendable supplies, and establishing a comfortable and inviting writers' environment.

Given the nature and extent of these duties, effective consultants can be hard to find. Many administrators of computer-supported writing facilities who go in search of professional, experienced consultants turn naturally to the staffs of departmental reading/writing centers. The tutors in these facilities— usually highly skilled and motivated writing instructors trained in supportive, one-on-one teaching skills—often make ideal

candidates for professional consultants in a computer-supported writing lab/classroom. Although reading/writing tutors
might require training in the use of computers, word-processing systems, and other technologically based duties, their
familiarity with writing research and theory and their lan-
guage-centered approach to teaching can assure a computer-
supported facility an appropriate focus on writing and the
teaching of writing.

Administrators can also turn to student populations for
professional writing/computer consultants. Some lab/class-
rooms, for instance, hire undergraduate English majors, or
graduate students in English and English education, and train
these individuals in necessary computer-related skills. This
approach, like the strategy of hiring professional reading/
writing tutors, allows an administrator to assemble a staff that
has a primary philosophical focus on language and writers
rather than on computers.

Other computer-supported writing facilities have reported
success in hiring undergraduate and graduate students major-
ing in technologically oriented programs—computer science,
information systems, or mathematics—who have a secondary
interest in writing or English-related studies. These students
bring expertise in technology to a lab/classroom but must be
trained in one-on-one teaching skills and process-based writing instruction. In ideal situations, of course, facility administrators have the budget and the flexibility to balance a staff of
consultants with individuals who have expertise in both writing instruction and computer technology.

Alternatives to hiring professional consultants also exist.
Administrators who do not enjoy the luxury of a large or stable
budget may have to depend on a volunteer staff of consultants
to oversee the daily operations of a lab/classroom. Generally,
volunteer consultants are students, with expertise in writing
or in computer technology, who are willing to share their
expertise with others. Although these students are not paid,
they can be reimbursed in a number of ways: with free use of
the lab/classroom computers for their own projects, with course

credit, with a letter of recommendation from a faculty administrator, and/or with invaluable teaching experience.

Often the composition of a staff of consultants will depend on a facility's budget. In ideal situations, labs are generously funded and can maintain a staff of professional consultants that provide consistent expertise in writing instruction and technological assistance. With limited funding, however, the option of employing professional consultants may be unavailable.

Facility administrators who enjoy minimal fiscal flexibility can try assembling a staff of consultants that combines the benefits of professionals and volunteers: hiring one or two part-time professional consultants who work with a larger staff of volunteer consultants. Under such a system, the professional consultants provide the consistency that a successful computer-supported writing facility needs and the volunteer consultants cover a large number of lab/classroom hours at little or no cost to the budget. If such a combined staff of professional and volunteer consultants is assembled carefully, it can function effectively with minimal help from an administrator. Professional consultants can take care of many of the day-to-day operational duties such as ordering supplies, training volunteer consultants, scheduling, and assigning tasks to be completed by each shift of consultants.

The task of training consultants, professional or volunteer, will depend to a great extent on the role they play in the lab/classroom. In some facilities, for example, consultants act as human security systems, watching to see that equipment and software stays put. In such cases, little formal training may be required. In other facilities, however, consultants are a much more valuable resource because they provide informal instruction in writing and computer technology. In such cases, training lab personnel involves a careful and consistent program of formal instruction.

These formal training programs can take many forms. Some are conducted by the facility administrator, some by a part-time professional consultant. Some are completed on-the-job, others as a prelude to hiring. Some involve training in the range of hardware and software products that are used in a facility; others stress the importance of providing effective process-based feedback for writers. Whatever the structure of a training program, it should be directly shaped by the instructional and operational goals of a computer-supported writing facility, a process that ensures a knowledgeable staff of consultants that can provide valuable support to an existing writing program.

Training the Staff of a Computer-Supported Writing Facility

For administrators who have been systematic about identifying the instructional and operational goals of a computer-supported writing facility, the task of developing an effective training program for consultants is relatively straightforward. Figure 4.1, for example, shows a self-paced training program that the lab/classroom administrator for our sample faculty might have developed.

Figure 4.1: Consultant Training Program

TRAINING PROGRAM FOR CONSULTANTS

Format:

— 9 self-instructional units in consultants' training notebook

— tests on each unit, administered by senior consultants, located in filing cabinet

— final certification (lab/classroom administrator)

Training supervisor: Senior consultants

Testing procedure:

— Tests can be administered by any senior consultant at the end of each instructional unit and readministered as needed until the consultant passes with a satisfactory score.

— Use the Consultants' Test Record Sheet to record, date, and initial all tests. Keep on file.

Description of Program:

UNIT #1: Complete four readings on process-based writing instruction.

Test: In writing, describe and justify two process-based strategies for helping writers generate ideas.

UNIT #2: Complete two readings on instruction and operation of the computer-supported writing lab/classroom.

Test: In the filing cabinet, locate handouts describing instructional and operational goals for an interested lab/classroom user.

UNIT #3: Complete the on-line introduction to the microcomputer (PC).

Test: Show a first-time lab/classroom user where to locate the on-line introduction disk and how to use it. Include the processes of turning on and off the PC, using the keyboard, and adjusting the screen controls.

UNIT #4: Complete the on-line tutorials for the word-processing package.

Test: Demonstrate, in the presence of a senior consultant, how to locate and use the on-line tutorials for the word-processing package.

UNIT #5: Practice and master the word-processing skills introduced in the on-line tutorials.

Test: Using the word-processing package, type and print out the model document for word-processing according to the directions. Submit results to a senior consultant for evaluation.

UNIT #6: Read the written documentation on the graphics package, the style-analysis package, and the invention software.

Test: Demonstrate, in the presence of a senior consultant, how to teach a student to locate and use the written documentation for these packages.

UNIT #7: Practice using the packages and documentation identified in UNIT #6.

Test: Demonstrate, in the presence of a senior consultant, how to teach a student to locate and use these software packages.

UNIT #8: Ask any certified consultant to demonstrate how to turn the printers on and off, load tractor-feed paper, change ribbons, change print wheels, and troubleshoot common printer problems.

Test: Demonstrate, in the presence of any certified consultant, the procedures listed above.

UNIT #9: Ask any senior consultant to demonstrate the procedures for reserving computer time for a student or a class, filing and replacing daily sign-up sheets at each computer, filing and replacing weekly schedule sheets, duplicating and formatting disks, and securing the lab premises at night.

Test: Demonstrate, in the presence of any certified consultant, the procedures listed above.

This example demonstrates how the specific training activities identified by our sample faculty grew directly from the instructional and operational goals they identified for their computer-supported writing lab/classroom in Figures 3.1 and 3.2. Consultants in such a program would get instruction in the process-based approach to composing that informs a department's existing writing program as well as the computer hardware and software that supports such an approach.

We suggest assembling training materials in a ring notebook that can be stored on a lab's/classroom's documentation shelf. Training materials assembled and stored in this fashion lend themselves to easy updating and access.

Considering Additional Technical Assistance

In most computer-supported lab/classroom settings, the administrators who oversee policy and the consultants who supervise daily operations have a minimal level of technical expertise in connection with computers. With such training, these people can handle much of the daily maintenance and repair of hardware and software. The time always comes, however, when major repairs or adjustments are needed. For these situations, administrators must generally arrange for some sort of technical support in connection with the lab/classroom.

Some computer-supported writing facilities rely on off-site technical support. Often this support is provided as part of a regular maintenance contract issued by a local hardware vendor or computer store. Other facilities arrange technical support through their school's academic computer services. Still others hire freelance experts chosen from the ranks of computer-science students or faculty. Often, as in other staffing-related matters, the facility director has limited choice in arranging for technical support. In such cases, school or institutional policy determines the kind of technical assistance to be used within a facility.

Of course, advantages and disadvantages exist for each arrangement. Maintenance contracts, for example, can be costly although they often provide the advantage of quick service. Academic computing services, usually offered free of cost by an institution, are frequently overburdened with requests and may consider a microcomputer lab/classroom devoted specifically to writing as a low priority in comparison to the campus mainframe. Freelance consultants work for a range of fees but also have a range of expertise that may affect their ability to solve a problem.

Lab/classroom directors who have their choice of technical-support resources should keep in mind three goals when arranging for technical-support staff.

1. Find a source of technical expertise that can provide hardware, software, and site applications specialists.

2. Seek consistency in technical personnel.

3. Hire technical specialists who are willing to communicate responsibly, honestly, and openly with specialists in the teaching of writing.

In the short sections that follow, we will explain the rationale for each of these suggestions.

SUGGESTION #1: Find technical experts that can provide help with hardware, software, and site applications.

The ideal source of technical support provides expertise in both hardware- and software-based problems and the particular applications of hardware and software used in a particular lab setting. Resources that cannot offer all three kinds of expertise generally produce more frustration than satisfaction.

One facility administrator experienced this frustration when she tried to correct a problem involving the sharing of a word-processing package among the twelve workstations on a single computer network. To get technical assistance, she ended up calling on three different sources of technical expertise—one that provided a hardware technician who checked out each of the personal computers that were part of the networked system, one that sent a software specialist to check on the word-processing software, and one that sent a networking specialist to examine the networking apparatus. Each of the technical experts came at different times, and each blamed the problem on a different component of the networked system. The hardware expert blamed the network software; the network specialist blamed the word-processing software; and the software expert blamed the hardware system. It was not until the lab/classroom director arranged a visit by a technical expert who was familiar with all three components of the system (the personal computers, the word-processing system, and the network) that she was able to solve the original problem.

SUGGESTION #2: Seek consistency in technical personnel.

Lab/classroom administrators will also want to choose a resource that can provide the same experts each time a problem occurs. Such an arrangement saves time and energy; if new experts come each time the facility experiences a problem, much valuable staff time is spent providing contextual information about the hardware-software systems that form the core of the facility. This approach also assures a consistency in maintenance and repair, and the advantages of such consistency are far reaching. Each person who works on a hardware or software system carries a special knowledge of that system—when, for example, a printer last malfunctioned or when a specific computer failed to boot properly. This contextual knowledge may be lost as increasing numbers of technical experts are called to service a facility. It is also important for administrators to know that each expert who works on a hardware or software system leaves a distinctive "footprint" on that system—a special way of programming the software to work on a piece of hardware or a certain way of repairing a piece of hardware. The more experts involved in the process, of course, the more footprints are left on the system and the more complicated that system becomes to work with in the future. Seeking consistency in the technical specialists who work with a given system will help minimize these difficulties.

SUGGESTION #3: Hire technical specialists who are willing to communicate honestly, openly, and responsibly with specialists in the teaching of writing.

Finally, lab/classroom administrators will want to seek technical experts who are willing and able to communicate with experts in the teaching of writing. Faculty who work long enough in a computer-supported writing lab/classroom are bound to encounter three kinds of technical experts that they should avoid: those who deliberately try to intimidate or confuse non-technical experts by using jargon-laden explanations, those who are incapable of explaining a problem in plain English, and those who are unwilling to deal with teachers of writing because these teachers insist that machines must take a secondary role to humans. These three kinds of technical experts can only make the job of administering or operating a computer-supported writing lab more difficult.

Of course, the composition experts on a lab staff—the director and the consultants—also have a central responsibility for sharing information in an honest and articulate fashion. In fact, unless members of a lab/classroom staff are familiar with the facility's instructional and operational goals that keep writing at the center of the program, they cannot succeed in helping the technical specialists—hardware technicians, software and applications experts, programmers—make the machines meet these goals.

Remembering Local Constraints

Although the information we have provided in this chapter can give an English faculty or a lab/classroom administrator a general idea of the personnel that might figure into the operation a computer-supported writing facility, such guidelines are necessarily subject to local constraints and specific college and university settings. Each institution, each department, and each faculty must deal with limitations and demands that cannot be generalized or predicted.

We do not want to suggest, therefore, that the personnel described within this chapter will be required or even desired in any given facility. Deciding on the staff needed to keep a lab/ classroom running smoothly usually involves a lengthy process of negotiation that begins with the planning of a facility and continues as that facility matures within a particular educational setting.

Chapter Five

Training Teachers to use a Computer-Supported Writing Facility

Designing a computer-supported writing facility is one thing; encouraging faculty to use it is another. Nothing is more disheartening to the administrator of a good lab/classroom than to see an expensive and carefully planned facility sitting empty for much of the day while faculty members hold their writing classes in traditional classrooms. But, unless a composition faculty can see the benefits of holding their writing-intensive classes in a computer-supported lab/classroom, no amount of careful planning and staffing will convince them to use such a facility. In most institutions and departments, a program of professional development is needed to inform teachers of the advantages of computer support for their writing-intensive classes. Often, such an educational effort is coupled with a training program in basic computer literacy.

In this chapter, we provide lab/classroom administrators with a series of practical suggestions for training English faculty in computer literacy and the effective use of computer-supported writing labs/classrooms. These suggestions are classified and explained in two parts. First, we discuss the issue of designing a training program in basic computer literacy; next, we talk about educating faculty in the use of a specific computer-supported writing facility.

Training Teachers to Use Computers: Lessons in Computer Literacy

Perhaps the best way to get English teachers to use a computer-supported writing lab/classroom is to "hook" them on using computers for their own professional work. In computer-literacy training programs, faculty are generally given a short introduction to a particular brand of computer and a word-processing package that runs on that machine. Some training programs also encourage or require individual teachers to check out computer equipment on which they can practice and master the skills they encounter in regularly scheduled group sessions. Additional exposure to spreadsheet packages, grade-book programs, spelling checkers, merge-print packages, or text-analysis programs also often are included in these training sessions.

Having all, or most, of the teachers on an English faculty acquire some form of computer literacy has several advantages, especially if such a program is carefully planned to encourage a shared basis of expertise. First, of course, are the benefits to individual teachers who are empowered with a knowledge of computers that is practical and immediately applicable to their own professional goals.

Second, come the benefits that accrue to a community of teachers. If the faculty and staff of an entire department or school can be introduced to a single brand of personal computer hardware and one word-processing package for their own work, they automatically will share a common system of computer-based communication. In such situations, intra- and interdepartmental communications are facilitated, secretaries and faculty can work on a single system, and the work done in a computer-supported writing lab can often be transported elsewhere within a college or department.

The third source of benefits from training programs in basic computer literacy involves computer-supported writing facilities. Teachers who use computers themselves, who know the strengths and weaknesses of these machines as they support writers' composing processes, are more likely to use a computer-intensive writing facility within a department and to be sophisticated and creative teachers within that facility. Basic training in computer literacy also eliminates redundant training by the staff of a computer-supported writing facility. If teachers can learn the same computer and word-processing package for professional purposes as they do in a computer-supported lab/classroom, both time and effort are saved.

Obstacles to Effective Training in Computer Literacy

Unfortunately, the process of training teachers in basic computer literacy is not always as easy as it sounds. English teachers can be reluctant about learning to use computers for a number of good reasons. First, such knowledge is, at least in one sense, naturally foreign to our field of study—most English composition teachers are trained, and inclined, to work with books, words, and language rather than with machines. In fact, up until the last few years, computers were seen as dehumanizing influences that had limited use in the study of oral and written language. Although this technophobia has become rarer in the recent past, its influence still persists in college- and university-level teacher-training curricula. Few English education programs at teacher-training institutions, for example, provide much formal and systematic instruction in using computers to support the teaching of English. Becoming literate with regard to computers is a task that many English composition teachers still have to undertake *after* they have secured their formal pedagogical training or finished their formal course of graduate study. Understandably, it is often difficult for these individuals to surrender the role of expert teacher and assume the role of naive learner.

A second reason that English teachers have, in the past, kept computers at a philosophical arm's length involves the language barrier that surrounds these machines. The culture of computer scientists and the culture of English teachers are separated by the linguistic metaphors that inform their differing realities. These disparate metaphorical realms make free and uninhibited exchanges between the groups difficult. People who design, manufacture, program, sell, maintain, and repair computers speak a different language than composition teachers—even though both groups claim to speak English—and teachers of writing often find this semantic wall too high or too linguistically slippery to clamber over. This language barrier can be a main source of the initial frustration that English teachers experience when they attempt to learn something about computers from computer specialists. The vocabulary of these specialists—rife with terms like RAM and ROM, hard disks and hardware, software and firmware, abort and execute, boot and bomb, load and crunch—is often so foreign in tone and meaning to teachers of English composition that these writing instructors experience linguistic alienation.

A third obstacle to computer literacy for English teachers has to do with the lack of specificity that characterizes many training programs. Although a number of colleges and universities now offer courses in computer literacy designed for faculty without prior technological experience, these courses often prove of limited value to English teachers. Such training programs offer a generic introduction to word-processing, data bases, and other utility programs, but this training seldom approaches the issue of computer literacy from the specific language-based perspective of an English composition teacher. Instructors within these generic programs, for example, may not be able to answer a writing teacher's questions about computer-assisted programs for invention and revision or to demonstrate the best bibliographical aids for scholars who contribute to MLA or NCTE publications. In addition, if these computer-literacy programs are taught by experts in computer science or slanted toward technological applications of computers, such programs can prove more frustrating than beneficial to English teachers.

Computer-Literacy Programs That Work for English Teachers

Not surprisingly, then, we can predict that the computer-literacy programs which *do* work best for teachers of English are designed by teachers of English and based on the specific needs of professionals in the field of English. If a college or university lacks an effective, centralized program for introducing faculty to basic computer literacy, the task of educating English faculty naturally falls within the purview of a computer-supported writing facility. If the staff members in these facilities already maintain a central focus on language and writing and enjoy a certain amount of computer expertise, they can generally be quite successful in designing programs that address the specific needs and experiences of English composition teachers.

Certainly, the instructional demands of creating an introductory program of computer literacy for English composition teachers are not exceptional in their fundamental content or structure. Training sessions, for example, as long as they focus on the needs of English teachers, can be of any format, duration, or structure. Typically, for an initial introduction to computers, most trainers concentrate on presenting a single word-processing package along with one or two other pieces of utility software. Introductory programs are also designed to include several sessions of limited duration, so that participants can have plenty of "hands-on" practice between formal training classes. Trainers often plan from two to six sessions (two to three hours each) or even more for an introductory series in computer literacy, depending on the expertise and motivation of the teachers in the training group.

In addition, introductory computer-literacy programs for English teachers can be offered in any format. These programs can involve instructional materials that are presented on video tape, in traditional notebooks, or on computer screens; sessions can involve a small or large group of faculty depending on the needs and interests of the department. Formal sessions for group training and informal practice sessions for individuals can be offered at any time of the day, depending on the schedules of participants. To provide for increased "out of class" practice time, English teachers who participate in such programs are often encouraged to "take out" computers for their office or home.

Nor must all computer-literacy programs for teachers of English involve group presentations or formal sessions and demonstrations. Some departments, for instance, prefer one-on-one introductions to computers and word-processing. In such programs, the staff of a computer-supported lab/classroom may be asked to offer individual tutorials for interested faculty members or to set up a program in which each teacher who learns a departmental word-processing program is required to teach another colleague the same skills. Typically, in such programs, a faculty member who wants to learn to use a computer for a specific project—writing a paper on Melville, for instance, or preparing class materials for an advanced composition course—initiates a request for training. The administrator of the department's computer-literacy program or computer-supported writing facility then assigns a peer tutor or staff tutor experienced in the use of the department's word-processing package. These "each-one-teach-one" programs have the advantage of flexible scheduling, individual motivation, and immediate application of the computer skills involved.

Whatever its content, structure, or format, however, a program of computer literacy for English teachers does have to be carefully planned and executed so that it addresses the professional needs and experience levels of participants in a specific way. In Figure 5.1, for instance, you can see how our sample faculty might have gone about planning their own initial program in computer literacy for English composition teachers.

Figure 5.1: Introductory Program in Computer Literacy for English Teachers

PURPOSE:

1. Provide faculty members who have had little or no computer experience an introduction to our personal computer workstation and experience with the basic capabilities of our word-processing software.

2. Acquaint English teachers with the advantages of word-processing software for professional activities.

FORMAT: 4 hour-and-a-half sessions (Monday, Wednesday, Friday, Monday); attendance voluntary.

INCENTIVES: New knowledge about computers and word processing; free use of personal computer for one academic term; 2 service credits

PERSONNEL: 2 senior consultants for every 10 faculty

EDUCATIONAL OBJECTIVES:

— To teach faculty the meaning of the following terms: workstation, CRT, disk drives, floppy disk, keyboard, CPU, printer, function keys, ENTER key, CTRL key, and ALT key.

— To teach faculty how to do the following tasks: turn a personal computer on and off, insert a floppy disk, adjust the brightness and contrast knobs, use the on-line tutorial for the personal computer workstation.

— To teach faculty how to use the two on-line tutorials that accompany the departmental word-processing software.

— To teach faculty how to compose, store, and print a short document using the word-processing software and the following specific skills: loading and accessing the word-processing software, inserting text, deleting text, setting margins, determining page format, naming and saving files, and printing files.

— To make faculty aware of the potential benefits of word-processing packages for teachers of English.

SESSION DESCRIPTIONS:

Session #1: Introduction to computer terminology and workstation

Session #2: Introduction to tutorials on word-processing software

Session #3: Practice with word-processing software. On the computer, brainstorm and list advantages of word-processing software for teachers of English. Print these lists, and discuss in small groups.

Session #4: Practice with word-processing software. On the computer, produce and print revised document about possible uses of word-processing packages for English teachers. Distribute copies of lists to participants.

This introductory program identifies two primary instructional goals: that teachers achieve a basic level of computer literacy and that they acquire the fundamental skills necessary for using a particular word-processing package. The instruction our sample faculty has planned also specifically addresses the professional interests and needs of English teachers. It is structured purposefully to make these teachers think about the uses of computers from an English teacher's point of view.

You might also notice a hidden agenda in this program. The program, because it is designed to take place within a departmental computer-supported writing facility, also accomplishes the task of introducing individual faculty members to the lab/classroom and some of the hardware and software it contains. The second half of this chapter expands on the importance of teacher-training efforts within a lab/classroom setting.

Training in computer literacy, of course, need not end with the completion of a single program. After offering introductory programs in computer literacy, many departments set up broader-based, more advanced programs of computer skills for English teachers. Generally, because such programs involve advanced training, they are voluntary in nature. Sessions in these programs frequently address particular kinds of computer applications of interest to English teachers, scholars, or researchers: different types of packages for word processing, software for indexing and bibliographic purposes, computer assistance for producing presentation graphics or mailing labels, and the use of computer-based statistical packages for the social sciences.

Advanced training programs in computer literacy may differ slightly from introductory programs. Although some of these follow-up programs are conducted during the academic year, most are held during summer months when faculty have more time for practicing sophisticated computer skills. Many of these longer programs also offer some sort of recompense for faculty who attend. In some college settings, and for some faculty, the advantages and satisfaction of new technological knowledge is considered to be sufficient repayment. Other programs offer participants stipends, access to personal computers, or service credits.

Training Faculty to use a Computer-Supported Writing Facility

Generally, English teachers who experience firsthand the advantages of using computers to support their own writing are quite willing to offer their students similar benefits in computer-supported writing classes. At this point, the administrator or staff of a computer-supported writing facility can offer faculty members important information in two areas: how to use the hardware, software, and services associated with a particular lab/classroom facility; and how to approach the unique challenges of planning, teaching, and focusing computer-supported courses in a writing-intensive curriculum.

Introducing Computer-Supported Writing Facilities

Most administrators of computer-supported writing facilities recognize the need to provide colleagues with some sort of introduction to the hardware, software, and systems included in a lab/classroom, although the content and form of such introductions vary widely from institution to institution, and from facility to facility. Some administrators, for instance, find it useful to make a general presentation about their lab/classroom at regular faculty meetings or colloquia, stressing the value of supporting writing-intensive courses within the English curriculum. Other administrators prefer to send out informational packets that give overviews of a facility's offerings (see Appendix A for an example of one such packet from one working lab/classroom). Still other administrators prefer to send out invitations that ask colleagues to drop by individually for an on-site introduction to a lab/classroom facility. In Figure 5.2, we have provided an example of such an invitation.

Figure 5.2: Invitation to an On-Site
Lab Orientation

MEMORANDUM

To: English Faculty
From: D. Lowery,
        Director Computer-Supported Writing Lab
Date: 12/18/87

Our department's new computer-supported writing lab/
classroom is now open for business!

We invite you to call or stop by for a personal tour of the
facility. Stay as long as you like; the lab staff will be happy
to explain exactly how the computers can support your own
professional projects and the writing-intensive classes you
teach.

Among other things, we can offer you support in the
following areas:

— learning word processing

— designing graphics on computers

— designing documents/layouts on computers

— preparing presentation graphics on computers

— making your handouts, syllabi, and lecture notes available on our computer network

— setting up an electronic peer-critique system

— setting up a computerized grading system

— using computers for large-scale correspondence and
  mailing projects

— using computers to teach writing-intensive classes

ABSOLUTELY NO COMPUTER EXPERIENCE NECES-
SARY! Come as you are.

Providing on-site orientation tours for English faculty members who respond to such invitations involves a special set of challenges for lab/classroom administrators. The content, length, and format of these orientations must be extremely flexible because they are entirely dependent on the audiences' expertise and interests. Generally speaking, lab orientations include one or more of the following components:

The facility: a general tour of the lab/classroom facility, including available hardware and software, documentation, filing and storage space, and work areas.

Scheduling: a discussion of how lab hours are scheduled, how the lab can be reserved for an entire class, and how individual students can reserve time in the lab.

Lab courses/fees: an explanation of any lab course or fee structure connected with the use of the facility.

Consultants: an introduction to the consultants who staff the lab/classroom, their expertise, and their duty hours.

Hardware/software/systems: a general explanation of how the hardware, software, and systems interact in the lab/classroom.

Hardware: a general introduction to the hardware workstations, including how to boot and turn off, use the keyboard, and adjust contrast and brightness knobs.

Word-processing software: a series of demonstrations or tutorials on the word-processing system used in the lab.

Other software: an explanation or demonstration of the software packages available for use in the lab/classroom and introduction to the tutorials and documentation connected with this software.

Class support: a discussion and/or demonstration of pedagogical support provided by the lab including such topics as using consultants as teaching assistants, storing lecture notes and handouts on computers, employing peer-feedback systems, using electronic mailboxes, taking advantage of large-screen projection systems, etc.

Philosophy: a discussion of the facility's instructional and operational goals, policies, rules, etc.

Of course, no one orientation session will include all of these components, and it is up to the facility administrator or staff to determine which components are needed for individual faculty or groups of faculty. In addition, lab administrators must realistically limit orientation programs in terms of available resources. Some administrators, for example, may prefer to offer group-orientation sessions for faculty with similar interests or levels of computer-related experience—an approach that can reduce the time-consuming commitment to individual orientations. Moreover, some administrators may want to leave orientation duties to senior lab consultants in an effort to reduce their own involvement in this task.

Helping Instructors Teach Computer-Intensive Classes

The responsibilities of some lab/classroom administrators end once faculty have been introduced to computers and the computer-supported writing facility. Other administrators have an additional responsibility for professional development; these individuals are generally directed to work with their colleagues in developing effective teaching strategies for courses that are held in a computer-supported lab/classroom.

Lab/classroom administrators involved in such projects will want to talk with teachers about how courses held in computer-supported writing classrooms differ from those held in traditional classrooms. Specifically, colleagues can explore three major differences:

— planning computer support for writing-intensive courses,

— teaching computer-supported writing classes, and

— focusing student effort within writing classes.

In the following sections, we suggest some of the topics and issues connected with each of these areas.

Planning Computer-Supported Writing Courses

Planning a computer-supported writing course at the college or university level, if it is done thoroughly and with attention to detail, is equally as difficult as teaching the course. In fact, given that most professionals in our field often have little or no experience in teaching with computer support, this task may even be more difficult than planning for traditional writing classes. Technology, in most cases, adds a new variable to the already complex equation of the classroom, and this variable can be negative as well as positive in its final effect.

Before adding a technological element to a writing course, therefore, faculty members should be convinced that such an addition will be beneficial. To this end, teachers who plan to add computer support to any particular course should ask themselves three questions before making a final decision:

PLANNING QUESTION #1: Will This Course be Improved by Computer Support?

One of the first lessons English teachers have learned in wrestling with curriculum design in the wake of the computer revolution is that computers are not right for every course, every teacher, or every student. In fact, unless the use of computers has distinct advantages for presenting course content, the additional work involved in redesigning a class may not be worth the effort.

A close look at the content and structure of a particular writing-intensive class will help teachers make this decision. Generally, writing classes that seem to benefit the most from computer support involve a great deal of writing and stress written assignments that can be done during the hours a lab/classroom is in operation. Classes that may not prove to be the best choices for computer support may require journal writes that are highly personal in nature, involve constant risk-taking in writing assignments, or stress the use of out-of-class field notes. Often, the writing done in such classes involves additional privacy requirements or on-the-spot writing that cannot be supported by semi-public labs/classrooms as they exist within most academic settings.

PLANNING QUESTION #2: How, and to What Extent, Should Computer Support be Used?

Integrating computer support into a writing-intensive class also involves defining an appropriate degree of computer engagement. Ironically, such definitions often prove complicated because of the wide range of choices available to teachers. Most departments, in designing a computer-supported writing facility, opt for maximum flexibility—creating computer-supported writing labs/classrooms that can accommodate large groups of students (for those teachers who choose to hold class sessions in the lab) or individual students (for teachers who prefer to let individuals use the lab during out-of-class hours).

This flexible lab/classroom set-up can be used in a number of ways. For some classes, a teacher may choose to conduct all class sessions in the lab/classroom and have every student use the computer-supported facility for all writing assignments. Such an arrangement assures that every class member and the teacher has consistent access to a common brand of computer, a common word-processing system, and a central location for electronically storing, retrieving, and sharing drafts of papers. For other classes, a single electronic exchange system is unnecessary. In these situations, teachers might prefer that students use the computer of their choice outside of regularly scheduled classroom hours. Generally speaking, course content, including the purpose and structure of specific writing assignments, should shape the extent of computer support for any given writing-intensive class.

PLANNING QUESTION #3: How Will Computers Change Writing Assignments in This Course?

Adding computer support to writing-intensive classes can change dramatically the assignments faculty give and the way in which these assignments are passed from instructor to student. Smart teachers plan for such changes before they happen.

In computer-supported classes, for example, writing assignments, and student responses to these assignments, never need to be printed in hard copy form—no dittos, no stencils, no photocopies need be produced. If a teacher chooses to experiment with this kind of electronic-exchange system, a whole series of planning activities must be completed before the class ever begins: the teacher must design and become familiar with the exchange system, writing assignments must be altered to include instructions on how to label electronic drafts, handouts must be put on a computer disk and catalogued, and class time must be allotted to train students in the use of the electronic-exchange system.

Teachers must also learn to reconsider the rhetorical nature of writing assignments delivered to the teacher via an electronic medium. Given the personal and speculative nature of students' journal entries, for instance, teachers may want to require individuals to store certain written assignments under secret passwords in invisible subdirectories or on a "private" floppy disk to protect them from unauthorized electronic eavesdroppers.

Finally, teachers should plan to rethink the strategies they will use for responding to students' written work—especially if the work will be graded on a computer screen rather than on a traditional hard copy. Instructors can plan, for example, to access students' work on a computer and, by changing the color of the type on the computer screen, display their responses to texts in a strikingly different color. Teachers might also want to experiment with displaying their responses in all capital letters (by pressing the CAPS LOCK key), displaying responses within the lines of a text (by using the INSERT key), or identifying particular student text components by making them blink or appear in a different color on the screen.

Teaching Computer-Supported Writing Courses

Although planning a computer-supported writing class can be a complicated matter involving considerations of presentation, course content, and course materials, such activities are only the initial trials that instructors will face. Teaching a computer-supported class is equally as challenging an undertaking. For, if the addition of computer support changes the way in which teachers have to prepare for their courses, this support also alters the way in which these classes are conducted—affecting the location of classes and the nature of class sessions themselves.

For example, when teachers decide to use the more intensive forms of computer support in their classes, they have to think differently about how specific class sessions would work and where they would best be conducted. Writing activities built around peer- or teacher-conference sessions, for instance, frequently lend themselves to the workshop atmosphere created in a good computer lab/classroom. Similarly, in-class and out-of-class critique sessions, brainstorming and sharing sessions, and demonstration sessions can often be presented more effectively using an electronically supported classroom than they can in a traditional classroom. For other writing-centered activities, however, teachers may require traditional class settings. Lectures, large-group discussions about out-of-class readings, or guest presentations, for example, may not be most effectively presented in a computer-supported facility.

Instructors who teach computer-supported, writing-intensive courses, especially those that meet regularly in a computer lab or classroom, must also learn that classes held within such a facility will differ in content from more traditional writing classes. Certainly, increasing the computer support in any particular course involves a commitment to increased discussion about the new writing technology. In a course, for example, in which students write their journal entries on the computer and the teacher responds to these journals electronically, the teacher may end up devoting five to ten minutes of each class period to a discussion of computer-related concerns. Students in such courses have to be told, for instance, how to label and date the electronic drafts they hand in so that the teacher can recognize these files; how to back up drafts so that they have "insurance" copies in case of an electronic failure; and how to guard their computer journals against electronic plagiarism.

In completely "paperless" courses, teachers generally end up devoting even more class time to discussions of technology. Students in such classes often have to be taught, for instance, how to exchange papers electronically, how to set up mailboxes on computer networks, how to use increasingly complicated software packages, or how to respond effectively to classmates' electronic drafts.

The time spent on such matters may be viewed both negatively and positively by teachers. During their early attempts at teaching computer-supported classes, instructors often resent time spent discussing writing technology—especially when they compare the already limited time available for discussing course content and writing itself. As teachers become more experienced in teaching such classes, however, two things often happen to change this attitude. First, instructors learn how to reduce the time devoted to the discussion of writing technology by refining the strategies of computer use within the framework of each class. They learn to communicate such strategies more efficiently to students, and to document techniques more effectively for the use of fellow teachers. Second, faculty come to realize that a knowledge of computer-supported writing skills is, in many cases, an essential component of students' education. These teachers recognize that computer-based strategies for manipulating and changing text files, protecting drafts, and using the computer to exchange information, are also valuable, process-oriented writing skills that individuals will need to survive in a world where writing and information sharing is technologically based.

This recognition becomes even more important when we realize that such skills are seldom part of a beginning course in computer literacy. Often, students come to writing classes knowing fundamental computer literacy skills (some programming, perhaps, or familiarity with a simple database or word-processing program) but not knowing how to take full advantage of the computer's power for more sophisticated text production, idea generation, concept manipulation, or document exchange.

Managing a Computer-Supported Writing Course

Teachers also must prepare themselves to learn lessons about managing computer-supported writing classes, especially those classes held occasionally or entirely in a computer lab/classroom. Teachers in traditional classrooms are familiar with an environment that minimizes distractions and maximizes focus on the teacher, but computer-supported environments are seldom amenable to such teacher-centered approaches.

In the traditional courses, the teacher stands at or near the front of the classroom, lectures or gives instructions for small-group discussions and activities, and enjoys a relatively high degree of control over students' attention. Little is present in traditional classrooms to distract students: teachers choose when to write on a chalkboard, when the students split into groups, and when those groups rejoin the larger class.

In a computer-supported classroom, a teacher-centered focus quickly dissipates. The physical layout of the computer classroom and the lure of the monitor screen are certainly two of the major factors that contribute to this change in focus. Many computer-supported writing classrooms across the country are set up with the computers facing each other in clusters so that students can collaborate freely as they work on their electronic writing. In a room without a real "front," with no podium or teacher's desk, teachers may initially feel lost. Contributing to this feeling is the difficulty of maintaining eye contact with students who sit behind a monitor.

An additional factor in classroom management proves to be the inviting nature of the blank computer screen. Teachers find, even with students who are most attentive in a traditional classroom setting, that the computer is a powerful attraction. Teachers who hold entire class sessions in a lab/classroom setting may find that their introductory remarks, tailored for the relatively sedate atmosphere and pace of a traditional classroom, are soon punctuated by keyboard sounds, first from one corner of the room and then from another as students are seduced into jotting phosphorescent messages on the monitor screens.

Attempts to guide an entire class through a computer-supported exercise can be equally fruitless. If twenty-five students start at the same point in an activity at the same moment, twenty-five will be at different stages of the activity at the next moment. Students with extensive computer experience sprint ahead, quickly discovering how to broadcast electronic messages to their peers after completing a task. Students without computer experience need extensive help from the teacher or their peers in understanding the technology to perform. Students somewhere in the middle experiment with the new writing technology and quickly leave their teacher in their dust. Added to this whirlwind of writing activity may be the clatter of twenty-five keyboards and multiple printers that can distract even the most flexible of teachers.

The end result is that some faculty members may be slow in learning to modify their instructional style when conducting a class in a computer classroom. They may find themselves lecturing less and circulating more among clusters of students seated at the computers. Teachers who use the lab/classroom must discover how to give concise directions about a computer-supported writing task—covering aspects of both the writing activity (purpose, audience, length, time limits, collaborative work) and the necessary components of the writing technology (file names, necessary word-processing strategies, the nature of electronic text exchange)—and then learn how to sit back and enjoy the writing energy around them.

Chapter Six

Training Students to use a Computed-Supported Writing Facility

In addition to faculty, students need additional training to make effective use of a computer-supported writing facility. Although most of our students now come to school with some expertise and familiarity with computers in general, they are seldom aware of how best to use these machines to support a process-based approach to writing. As a result, they may find the task of using computers effectively in an English composition course to be more difficult than anticipated.

This chapter provides some practical suggestions for teaching students to use computers to support their efforts in writing-intensive classes. The suggestions are broken down into two basic categories: teaching students how to use computers, and teaching students how to succeed in computer-supported writing courses.

Teaching Students How to Use Computers

Perhaps the most common complaint associated with teaching computer literacy is that it takes time. Most English composition faculty feel that the process of teaching and learning computerized writing strategies takes up the valuable classroom hours that could be spent teaching and learning writing strategies or critical reading skills.

In fact, some English departments and faculties refuse to teach such skills, preferring instead to let students obtain basic skills through college-wide computer-literacy courses. These courses, however, seldom teach students the specific computer skills they need to succeed in a computer-supported writing class. Often, college-wide computer-literacy courses provide students with a smattering of programming skills (which they do not need in a process-based writing class), an introduction to a word-processing package (which often differs from the word-processing package these students use for their writing-intensive classes), and some rudimentary knowledge about the computer as a machine (which may or may not be essential to the task of using computers as writing tools). At the end of these courses, students may still not know how to manipulate organizational elements of a text electronically, how to effectively create electronic drafts, or how to use the computer's power for invention and planning activities when writing.

As a result of these shortcomings, many English teachers and departments, especially those that have access to computer-supported writing facilities, prefer to design and conduct their own programs of computer education for students. In some educational settings, for instance, individual English faculty provide basic instruction in computer skills, each faculty member covering only those skills needed for his or her own writing-intensive class.

Several advantages are associated with this approach. First, such a program assures that all students in writing-intensive classes receive the necessary instruction in computer-supported composing strategies but protects any one individual writing teacher from shouldering the entire burden of computer literacy. Moreover, this type of computer-literacy effort focuses on computer-supported *writing* strategies in a specific sense rather than *computer* skills in general. Because each English teacher addresses only those computer skills students need for completing the writing assignments involved in a particular course, specific technological applications are directly integrated with composition instruction. For example, only those teachers who want their students to share drafts on an electronic network are expected to explain the structure and use of a network in their classes. Other teachers who may want to use only a word-processing application and share drafts in disk form need not instruct their students on the use of a network system but must provide instruction in disk swapping and file manipulation. Distinct disadvantages are also connected with such a computer-literacy system, however. This approach does nothing, for example, to address English teachers' objections about sacrificing class time in writing courses to instruction in computer skills. In addition, the burden of instruction in such programs is not always equitably assumed by all members of an English faculty. Teachers of introductory writing classes, for instance, usually end up taking more of their class time to teach initial computer literacy while teachers of advanced writing courses reap the benefits of students who have enjoyed previous basic training.

As an alternative to asking individual faculty members to instruct students in computer skills, some English composition programs offer computer-literacy courses taught by the staff members of computer-supported writing facilities. These courses, which vary widely in the amount and duration of the instruction they offer, are often designed as prerequisites for writing-intensive classes within a school or department and, as such, are offered frequently or constantly throughout an academic year.

Computer-literacy programs offered through a computer-supported writing facility have distinct advantages. First, like the literacy instruction provided by individual English teachers, these programs maintain a focus on computer-supported *writing* strategies rather than on *computer* skills in general. Hence, these courses can offer students more sophisticated and focused instruction in using the computer effectively as a powerful writing technology. For example, there is some evidence that students left to their own devices fail to use the many features of word-processing programs. Instead of taking full advantage of block moves for deletion and rearrangement of text, they rely on the single delete key and often retype text needlessly. Other evidence suggests that writing at computers differs from writing with pen and paper. Point-of-utterance revision, for example, is difficult to distinguish from initial drafting, and strategies for planning may also change with technology. Thus, it behooves writing teachers and computer-supported writing facilities to offer computer-literacy courses that introduce students to a full repertoire of word-processing activities and to alert them to possible differences between the two modes of composing. Without this preparation, some students will never take full advantage of the unique features of computers. Unlike instruction offered by individual teachers, however, these courses have the additional advantage of standardizing the instruction every student receives and coordinating computer-literacy efforts through a central staff member. Thus, all teachers of writing-intensive classes in an English program can assume a minimal level of computer expertise on the part of all students who take such a course. Individual English teachers, for instance, need not worry about providing training in the fundamentals of word processing, file manipulation, or disk handling. Second, because these courses are taught by the staff of a computer-supported writing facility and are not part of any one class, they do not subtract from the time faculty members have to teach writing.

These courses do, of course, have disadvantages as well. Because they often carry minimal credit or no credit at all for enrollment, students can only be expected to master the fundamental skills associated with computer-assisted writing. Specialized computer skills associated with more complex and sophisticated areas of document design or graphics production may still need to be taught in individual writing-intensive classes. Departments also have to be careful about the philosophical focus in these courses, making sure that technological expertise is well balanced by pedagogical expertise and general familiarity with the instructional goals of a writing program.

Finally, in lieu of offering a single standardized course in computer literacy, some English departments rely on the staff of a computer-supported writing facility to provide a whole range of computer education classes tailored specifically for different types of writing-intensive courses. Thus, the computer education offered to students in a creative writing course might vary from that offered to students in an English literature class. Such an arrangement, for example, can accommodate both the teacher of a first-year composition course who decides that he or she wants students to learn the basics of a word-processing package and the teacher of an advanced journalism course who decides that students need to learn a sophisticated software package for page-layout activities. Most often for such programs, classes are scheduled separately in the computer lab/classroom for one or two sessions at the beginning of the term and instructed by lab personnel. In some settings, this arrangement still requires that teachers devote a class period or two, in the early weeks of a course, to technology. In other settings, students' schedules are more flexible and large-group instructional visits can be arranged outside of regular class hours.

Approaching Instruction in Computer Literacy

Even given their diversity of design, computer-literacy programs created by different English faculty for specific student populations share some common instructional approaches. An overview of these approaches, which can be built around traditional presentation formats as well as electronic instructional aids, can be generally helpful to educators faced with designing and implementing computer-literacy programs.

On the following pages, we present such an overview, but with a note of caution much like that which should precede any educational advice from a single source. No one program of computer literacy will, or indeed should, be designed to include all of the approaches listed in this overview. In fact, on behalf of students who must learn important computer-supported writing skills under already difficult circumstances, we suggest avoiding "bells and whistles" whenever possible. Rather, we encourage individual English teachers, armed with a thorough knowledge of their own students and of the computer facilities within which they work, to evaluate the relative merits of each instructional approach and to decide which components will be most useful within specific educational settings.

Lecture/discussion/practice: Like any other subject matter, computer-based writing skills can be taught using a presentation-practice sequence. Such an approach, in which the teacher presents oral information on a particular skill and then students discuss and practice that skill, is easily adapted to one-on-one tutorials, small-group instructions, or whole-class presentations on computer-based writing skills.

Hard-copy documentation: Many faculty members find that the manuals and paper-based training materials accompanying software packages or hardware systems serve as valuable instructional tools in computer-literacy courses. These materials—which include hard-copy tutorials, reference manuals, keyboard templates, workbooks and worksheets, exercises, peek sheets, etc.—can be used to support any approach to teaching computer-based writing skills.

On-line documentation: Some companies prefer to put instructional documentation for software packages or hardware systems on a computer screen so that users become quickly adapted to the medium of the cathode ray tube. Such materials—which include on-line tutorials, help screens, keyboard simulations, or guided tours of software packages or hardware systems—can also serve as useful instructional tools in computer-literacy courses. Often teachers choose to use on-line documentation supplemented by hard-copy materials in training situations, thus allowing increased flexibility for accommodating students with preferences for specific media.

On-line instructional materials sometimes take advantage of the computer's ability to produce limited animation and other graphic aids. In addition, some on-line documentation is controlled by the learner (i.e., the user determines when to move to the next screen or what to do next). Other on-line material is programmed to proceed without learner control. The amount of learner control a particular set of on-line materials offers may influence a teacher's decision regarding training.

Cassette-tape materials: Audio tapes are often used in conjunction with on-line introductions to software packages or hardware systems. In connection with a word-processing package, for instance, a taped audio narrative may help explain the action that occurs in an on-screen demonstration of text-block moves. These tapes can also be used in connection with hard-copy materials. The staffs of some labs/classrooms, for example, introduce students to their facility by providing training materials that combine audio-taped and hard-copy instructions. Audio-taped training materials may be especially important for student writers who are visually impaired.

Videotape materials: Some teachers prefer using videotaped materials to introduce students to hardware systems or software products. Frequently, videotapes involve enlarged screen displays and may be keyed to supplementary on-line or hard-copy documentation.

Large-screen displays: Schools that have access to large-screen computer display systems frequently use them to teach students how to use software packages or hardware systems. With this medium, teachers can project an image of a computer screen that is large enough for an entire class to see at one time.

Although many of the instructional aids mentioned in the preceding list are available through commercial vendors, versions of them can also be created by individual English faculty or the staff of a computer-supported writing facility and thus tailored for a particular educational environment and student population. The staff of many labs/classrooms, for example, rewrite all hard-copy documentation that comes with products to eliminate computer jargon or to appeal to a special target audience. Other labs have developed their own guided-tour cassette tapes that "walk" students through the initial steps of learning a word-processing package or have made videotapes that show the potential uses of a particular graphics package.

Designing Computer-Literacy Instruction for Students

Regardless of the particular instructional strategies chosen for teaching computer-based writing skills, regardless of the particular student population, and regardless of whether literacy instruction is designed collectively by an English department or individually by a faculty member, literacy training must still be done. Although the range of possible instructional situations precludes overly specific guidance, we can suggest two general caveats for designing such training programs.

First, individual computer-literacy programs for students should be shaped by the same processes of planning and design advocated throughout this book. Thus, the overall goals of such programs should be directly and immediately informed by the goals of the larger English composition program that supports the training, shaped by what a faculty knows about writing and the teaching of writing. Individual training activities, as well, should be influenced by an English program's philosophical values. Maintaining this focus on writing and writers rather than on computers whenever possible during a computer-literacy training process will help teachers determine which computer instruction is most directly applicable to the instruction that goes on within particular writing-intensive classes.

Second, computer-literacy programs presented in computer-assisted writing labs/classrooms should involve the same careful and systematic pedagogical planning that goes into any other class. Teachers or staff members in charge of training efforts should identify the purpose of each lesson within a computer-literacy program, the specific audience to which the lesson will be taught, the learning objectives for every instructional unit, and the best format for materials to be used in that unit. Some labs/classrooms, in fact, develop detailed lesson plans for each instructional unit that they teach. Figure 6.1 represents a lesson plan that might have been designed in the computer-supported writing lab/classroom of our sample faculty.

Figure 6.1: Lesson Plan for Computer-Literacy Session

PURPOSE: To teach students how to use a word-processing package as an invention aid.

AUDIENCE: First-year composition students in process-based writing courses.

REQUIRED EXPERIENCE: Students must already be able to perform five basic tasks in connection with our word-processing package: creating a file, inserting and deleting text, saving a file, and recovering a file.

INSTRUCTIONAL OBJECTIVES:

1. After creating a file called INVENT.LST, students will be able to brainstorm a list of at least 15 topics for a paper (any topic).

2. Students will be able to choose their favorite topic from those topics on their original list.

3. Using the block-save function, students will be able to send the remainder of their ideas to a separate word-processing file (SAVE.REF) for later reference.

4. Using the original file containing their favorite topic (INVENT.LST), students will be able to brainstorm a list of at least 15 key words/ideas associated with this topic.

5. After being shown the add-a-line function of the word-processing package, students will be able to complete a five-minute freewrite on 6 out of the 15 key words/phrases they have identified in connection with their topic.

6. Using the delete function, students will delete those key words they consider extraneous to their emerging paper topic.

7. Using the block-move function to experiment with different organizational arrangements of the freewrites and key words, students will produce at least three different documents.

FORMAT: Demonstration and practice session in the computer lab.

MATERIALS: Hard-copy documentation of the following functions: add line/word, delete line/word, block-move, block-save.

LENGTH: 1 hour

Of course, the use of specific instructional approaches and teaching aids will differ according to the material being covered in a particular literacy program and the student population for which the program is being designed.

Surviving in a Computer-Supported Writing Class

Students who have developed strategies for succeeding in a traditional writing classroom may not automatically succeed in a computer-supported writing classroom. In fact, just as teachers must learn new ways of planning, teaching, and evaluating courses taught in a computer-supported environment, students must learn new strategies for coping with the same environment.

Given this situation, some English composition teachers feel an ethical responsibility to teach their students strategies that go beyond the scope of computer-literacy classes as we have described them thus far. Although different faculty members handle this process in different ways, some.basic suggestions might help students profit from any computer-supported writing class. We have detailed just a few such suggestions in the following list:

SUGGESTION #1: Explore, explore, explore.

In a traditional writing class, you (the student) turn to books, journals, a library, or the teacher for help as you are composing. In a computer-supported writing class, these resources are still available, but you also have some additional help if you need it. Spend some time exploring the various kinds of computer documentation or tutorials (hard-copy, on-line, videotape) available for your writing-intensive class. Learn to find specific kinds of help (hard-copy documentation, on-line documentation, audio-tape documentation, etc.) within the computer facility you will be using. Also, become familiar with any consultants who might be available to help you. Take systematic notes on questions you have that involve using the computer. Ask your teacher or the consultant for assistance with these questions.

SUGGESTION #2: Practice, practice, practice.

Before you try using a piece of computer equipment or a new software package for an important writing assignment that you have to hand in, practice on a less important project. Take notes on any problems you encounter and mention these to the consultants and to your teacher. Use this first "pilot" project you complete on the computer to work out the serious problems you are bound to encounter when learning to use a new technology.

SUGGESTION #3: Save your work frequently, and back up all files.

Blessed are the students who make backups of important work, for they have adequate insurance. Computers, software, and systems frequently suffer from sudden electronic glitches that can wipe out the hard work you have done. To protect against accidental loss of files, save your work frequently (some software does this automatically) and keep a separate backup disk. Update this backup disk at the end of every working session; it is your insurance policy.

SUGGESTION #4: Get to know your word-processing package.

Be creative in your use of the computer's word-processing power. Use the word-processing support available to you to make class work easier. If possible, store your lecture notes and reading notes on the computer. Typing these notes from their original handwritten form will help you remember material, and the typed notes will be easier to review when you are studying for a test. If class is held in a computer-lab setting, try taking your notes directly on the computer—you may find this process faster than handwriting. Use the word processor to practice essay exam questions and to store practice answers; then, study the questions and answers when reviewing for a test.

Section Three

Improving a Computer-Supported Writing Facility

Chapter Seven

Keeping Records in a Computer-Supported Writing Facility

Any administrator or faculty member who has worked in or around a computer-supported writing facility can attest to the value of keeping careful records. Such activities prove especially important within a computer-supported lab/classroom for several reasons: the relatively recent appearance of computers as an expense item on the budgets of English departments and writing programs, the complex nature of a computer-supported writing facility as a pedagogical operation, and the increasing need to identify the effects of computers on writers and the teaching of writing. This chapter briefly discusses these contributing factors and then outlines the various kinds of records that lab/classroom administrators might find it helpful to keep.

Why Keep Records?

As noted earlier in this book, the use of computers as writing tools is a relatively new phenomenon. If computer use itself is at an early stage of development, then our profession's firsthand experience with designing and administering large-scale computer-supported writing facilities is positively embryonic. Only recently, for example, have English teachers and their students pressed schools for computer facilities designed specifically with writers in mind. Only recently have department and writing-program administrators been able to visit established computer-supported writing facilities to determine how such a lab/classroom might benefit their faculty, students, and academic communities. Finally, it is only recently that administrators have had to face the twin challenges of justifying and funding the design, implementation, and continuing operation of computer-supported writing facilities. It is this last point that underscores the need for careful recordkeeping on the part of lab/classroom teachers and administrators.

Although the practice of justifying instructional needs and accounting for expenditures is not an unfamiliar activity for department heads and program administrators, the necessity of doing so in connection with computers is. Complicating this task is the fact that serious research in the field of computer-assisted writing instruction has, at this point, produced minimal empirical evidence that precisely identifies the benefits of computers for writers. Thus, our profession provides administrators little in the way of "ammunition" to justify the large initial capital expenditures or the large continuing budgets that such facilities require. To fill this void, lab/classroom administrators must be encouraged to keep accurate and exhaustive records within the context of specific computer-supported writing programs, records that tell how much facilities cost to establish (in terms of equipment, software, and personnel), how much to operate (on a daily and yearly basis), and how much they are used (by faculty, staff, and students).

A second important reason for keeping records involves our continuing professional obligations. Until careful records are kept in established labs/classrooms, our profession will remain ignorant of the essential questions in connection with computers and writing: What impact does computer technology have on writers, their writing processes, and the texts these writers produce? What can teachers of writing do to make our current use of computers more effective? How can lab/classroom administrators create inviting and productive computer environments that support writers and their efforts? To answer these questions and others, administrators, teachers, and staff must keep records of instructional evaluations (which attempt to pinpoint the impact of technology on students and teachers), facility evaluations (which identify the effectiveness of existing documentation, consulting staff, operational procedures, software, and hardware), and research projects completed within the context of working labs/classrooms.

What Records Should We Be Keeping?

Unfortunately the answer to the preceding question could take a book in itself to detail. Most lab/classroom administrators find that the more records they keep, the better their lab/classroom functions. Although collecting and analyzing data from records is time consuming, carefully accumulated information helps justify expenditures, improves instruction, wards off frustration, and makes labs/classrooms better places to teach and learn. The following pages provide a partial listing of the kinds of records existing labs/classrooms keep and some examples of forms that might be helpful for collecting recordkeeping data.

RECORDKEEPING SUGGESTION #1: Budgets

Not many English teachers are also financial wizards, but accurate figures on expenditures are of central importance in the continuing operation of a computer-supported writing lab/ classroom. Administrators frequently ask for data describing the cost of lab/classroom operations—by the semester or the year. Budget forms for computer-supported writing facilities may need to detail some or all of the following costs:

—personnel: salaries for writing consultants, computer technicians, and lab/classroom administrators

—hardware and equipment: cost of computers, printers, peripherals, upgrades, vacuum cleaners, etc.

—software: purchase of new packages, upgrades, auxiliary packages, additional documentation, etc.

—expendable supplies: cost of paper, ribbons, print wheels, screen wipes, disks, toner cartridges for laser printers, etc.

—repair and maintenance: expenses involving repair, cleaning, site and system maintenance, etc.

Figure 7.1 and 7.2 show two forms that a lab/classroom might want to keep in connection with budget reports: a term-by-term expense worksheet, which shows categories of expenditures and personnel costs, and a term budget report that balances facility costs against income.

We suggest copying and modifying these forms to fit the needs of your particular computer-supported writing facility, faculty, staff, and students.

RECORDKEEPING SUGGESTION #2: Evaluations

At some point, most directors of computer-supported writing facilities are asked to assess the instructional effectiveness of their operation. Although there are any number of evaluations

Figure 7.1: Sample Term-By-Term Expense Worksheet

TERM EXPENSE WORKSHEET:
Winter Term (10 weeks), 1987-88

Description	P.O. #	Items	Cost
HARDWARE EXPENSES			
Purchases	IB08007	Network Translator Kit	$ 444.72
Repairs	IB08013	Diablo Inkjet Printer	$ 284.71
Maintenance	IB08017	Headcleaning	
		kits (ACS)	$ 23.86
Total Hardware Expenses			$ 753.29
SOFTWARE EXPENSES			
Purchases	PO10537	Hayden Speller (1)	$ 37.75
	IB08175	Turbo Pascal (1)	$ 32.00
	PO12598	Volkswriter 3 (5)	$ 300.00
Total Software Expenses			$ 369.75
EXPENDABLE SUPPLIES			
Purchases	IB08017	Disks	$ 284.50
	IB08017	Paper	$ 167.29
	PO12252	Printwheels/thimbles	$ 62.48
	IB08199	Ribbons	$ 875.25
	IB01072	Name tags	$ 3.75
Total Expendable Expenses			$1393.27

Personnel Salaries	Wage	Cost
Administrator	$3000.00/qrt	$3000.00
Consultants		
Jones	40hrs/wk X 10 wks @	
	$ 3.50/hr	$1400.00
Pauley	40hrs/wk X 10 wks @	
	$ 4.00/hr	$1600.00
Total Personnel Expenses		$6000.00
TOTAL EXPENSES	WINTER 1987-88	$8516.31

Figure 7.2: Sample Term Budget Report

TERM BUDGET REPORT:
Winter Term (10 weeks), 1987-88

Income

Number of student lab/classroom fees @ $20.00		$ 300.00
Income generated by païd-student users		$ 8200.00

Expenses

Number of part-time personnel	2	
Salaries of part-time personnel		$3000.00
Salaries of administrators		$3000.00
Hardware Expenses		
Purchase	$ 444.72	
Repair	$ 284.71	
Maintenance	$ 23.86	
		$ 753.29
Software Expenses	$ 396.75	
		$ 396.75
Expendable Supplies		
Disks	$ 284.50	
Paper	$ 167.29	
Printwheels	$ 62.48	
Ribbons	$ 875.25	
Miscellaneous	$ 3.75	
		$1393.27
Total Expenses		$8543.31
Profit		
Deficit		$ 143.31

from which to choose, facility directors may want to consider at least three important sources of evaluative data:

1) student-generated evaluations of computer-supported writing facilities or classes,

2) consultant-generated evaluations of lab/classroom operations, and

3) teacher-generated evaluations of the instructional services in a lab/classroom.

Student-generated evaluations can reveal important information about how users rate a facility's value as a writing environment, as well as its atmosphere, capacity, users' fees, and instructional efforts. Figure 7.3 represents a student-generated evaluation that touches on some of these topics.

**Figure 7.3: Student Generated Lab/Classroom
Survey**

USER SURVEY
Center for Computer-Assisted Language Instruction (CCLI)

1. Rate the usefulness of the CCLI for the writing tasks you do:

Low   Medium   High
|————————————————|————————————X————|

Comments: I couldn't write without a computer now. But what happens when the power goes out?
2. Rate the atmosphere in the CCLI:

Low   Medium   High
|————————————————|————————X————————|

Comments: I know you want writers' groups to work in the lab, but sometimes it gets too noisy.

3. Why are you using the CCLI? (circle one)

school writing   personal writing   all writing

other:_____

4. What part did your instructor play in getting you to use the CCLI?
   (circle one)

suggested   strongly urged   required

other:_____

5. What would make the CCLI a better writer's environment?
   Please comment on the back of this sheet.

6. Have you ever had to wait in line to use a computer in the CCLI?
   Please comment on the back of this sheet.

7. What is the most valuable part of the CCLI for you? The consultants? The computers? The instruction in word processing?
   Please comment on the back of this sheet.

8. What new software and/or hardware does the CCLI need most?
   Please comment on the back of this sheet.

Consultant-generated evaluations can provide an "insider's" view of lab/classroom operations. Such reports often focus on self-evaluations of teaching effectiveness, facility needs, student requests, procedural weaknesses and strengths. Figure 7.4 represents an open-ended, consultant-generated evaluation.

Teacher-generated evaluations are valuable in summarizing the instructional support services that a lab/classroom provides. Faculty can be asked to summarize the services of which they avail themselves or indicate which services they find most effective, to list equipment or software that they need for their teaching, and to identify procedures that have negative or positive impacts on their instruction. Figure 7.5 represents a faculty questionnaire that Michigan Tech has employed for purposes of obtaining recordkeeping data.

**Figure 7.4: Consultant-Generated
Lab/Classroom Evaluation**

CONSULTANT'S EVALUATION

1. What things are we doing best in this lab/classroom? Among other activities, consider writing instruction, one-on-one tutoring, documentation, security, creating a writers' environment, computer literacy for students, computer literacy for teachers, etc.

   Our one-on-one and small-group instruction in computer literacy and word processing for students is fine—we're doing a good job there. Also, I think we do a bang-up job teaching document-design packages on the Mac.

2. What things do we need to work on? Among other activities, consider writing instruction, one-on-one tutoring, documentation, security, creating a writer's environment, computer literacy for students, computer literacy for teachers, etc.

   We *still* aren't reaching some of the teachers—especially the computer phobes on the faculty. We're also busting at the seams, so the writers don't have enough room to spread out their papers or just to sit around and talk. Can't we knock out the east wall?

3. In what areas do you, personally, want additional training? Consider writing instruction, one-on-one tutoring, documentation, security, creating a writer's environment, computer literacy for students, computer literacy for teachers, etc.

   I need *help* on block moves, concatenation, and layouts in Volkswriter 3!

Figure 7.5: Faculty Generated Lab/Classroom Evaluation

1. For what classes are you currently using the lab/class-room? Identify each class, briefly describe the way in which you use computers, and rate the support services we provide—all on the chart below:

Class	Description of Use	Rating (1-5)
ENG101	Whole class meets in lab/classroom on group-critique days, 8 times per term	5
ENG305	Students use lab/classroom on individual basis	4

2. What things do we do best for your classes?

   The network system allows my students in the first-year composition course to exchange drafts of papers under their pen-names and receive immediate feedback from individuals in a peer-critique group. I really like this system. The feedback is much more honest. I respond under a pen-name, too, so that authors will take all comments equally as seriously.

3. What do we need to do differently?

   Bar students from using those headsets and radios when they write in the lab/classroom. They zombie out.

4. Are there any services we *do not* provide that you would like to see?

   Yes, can we have a faculty-development session on merge print packages? I need it for a publicity mailing.

RECORDKEEPING SUGGESTION #3: Lab Use Data

Data on the amount of use a computer-supported writing facility gets are essential in shaping on-going operations and planning for future operations. Many labs keep detailed records that include term-by-term information on topics such as the following: total hours and average hours used by students/faculty/staff, total hours and average hours used by particular classes/majors/projects, and total hours and average hours of use for each computer and for all computers.

Several reporting forms are needed to collect and analyze all this data, and each lab/classroom facility will find it valuable to design such forms to reflect local operational and instructional goals. Sometimes, however, it can help to see how comparable facilities are accomplishing the recordkeeping task. So, we have provided several lab-use forms that seem to work well for Michigan Tech's facility. At the basic recordkeeping level, in Figure 7.6, we have included a sign-up sheet that provides data on individual machine use and the nature of computer-assisted projects. Figure 7.7 represents a weekly tally sheet used to collect data for each computer in the facility, and Figure 7.8 represents an end-of-term tally sheet used to compile this weekly data in a form more convenient for later reference.

RECORDKEEPING SUGGESTION #4: Personnel Schedules

Some lab/classroom administrators find it useful to keep records on the number of hours various writing consultants, computer technicians, teachers, lab staff, or administratorsspend in support of a facility. Such information can prove useful in justifying new or continuing positions. Figure 7.9 shows a staff schedule chart that MTU's facility employs to keep track of such data.

Those labs/classrooms which involve a number of different people in daily operations also may find it useful to keep track of what went on during each employee's shift. Such information often proves valuable in making sure that the lab is

Figure 7.6: Sign-up Sheet

CENTER FOR COMPUTER ASSISTED LANGUAGE INSTRUCTION
COMPUTER_____

Date	Time in	Time out	Major	Project or Class	Name	Student? (S) Consultant? (C) Faculty (F)

computer s gnup table

Figure 7.7: Weekly Tally Sheet

WEEKLY TALLY SHEET
Week: (Circle) 1 2 3 4 5 6 7 8 9 10

Date: From:_____   To:_____

Computer	HU 011 Students	Faculty/ Consultant Use	Classroom Use	Total Hours
A				
B				
C				
D				
E				
F				
G				
H				
I				
J				
K				
L				
M				
N				
O				
P				
Q				
R				
S				
T				
U				
V				
W				
X				
Y				
Z				
Total IBMs				
Mac-A				
Mac-B				
Total Macs				
TOTAL				

Figure 7.8: End-of-Term Tally Sheet

QUARTERLY TALLY SHEET

QUARTER: (Circle) FALL   WINTER   SPRING   SUMMER

DATE: From_____ To_____

	Week	HU 011 Students	Faculty/ Consultant	Classroom Use	Total
IBMs	1				
	2				
	3				
	4				
	5				
	6				
	7				
	8				
	9				
	10				
	Exam Week				
TOTAL					
MACs	1				
	2				
	3				
	4				
	5				
	6				
	7				
	8				
	9				
	10				
	Exam Week				
TOTAL					
GRAND TOTAL					

Figure 7.9: Staff Schedule Chart

Staff Schedule
Winter '87-88

	SUN.	MON.	TUES.	WED.	THUR.	FRI.	SAT.
8-9		Mary Ann Martin	Gereld Kocan	Mary Ann Martin	Gerald Kocan	Mary Beeby	
9-10		Mary Ann Martin		Steph Sines	Lisa Sporleder	Mary Beeby	
10-11		Liz Smith	David Macaulay	Liz Smith	Lisa Sporleder	Mary Beeby	Kevin Williams
11-12	R. Stone	Gerald Kocan	Macaulay/ Finlayson	Gerald Kocan	Leslie Finlayson	Gerald Kocan	David Borrillo
12-1	R. Stone	Donna Zalensas	Leslie Finlayson	Donna Zalensas	Leslie Finlayson	Donna Zalensas	Borrillo Purczynski
1-2	R, Stone	Bob Yeo	Curry/ Young	Jim Curry	Yeo/ Young	Julie McIlvenny	Yeo/ Purczynski
2-3	R. Stone	Bob Yeo	Jim Curry	Julie McIlvenny	Gerald Kocan	Julie McIlvenny	Yeo/ Purxzynski
3-4	R, Stone	Hester Butler	Fritz Kuehnel	Susan Maloney	Macaulay Collins	Brenda Mayo	Jack Hedenberg
4-5	Kevin Williams	Hester Butler	Fritz Kuehnel	Susan Maloney	Margo Collins	Brenda Mayo	Jack Hedenberg
5-6	Lisa Spranger	Hester Butler	Fritz Kuehnel	Susan Maloney	Margo Collins	Brenda Mayo	Jerry Brownell
6-7	Lisa Spranger	Lisa Spranger	Dan Ehle	David Borrillo	Julie McIlvenny		
7-8	Becky Hoppe	Jerry Brownell	Dan Ehle	Jenny Hagy	Amy Bronson		
8-9	Becky Hoppe	Jerry Brownell	Amy Bronson	Jenny Hagy	Amy Bronson		
9-10	Becky Hoppe	Jack Hedenberg	Steph Sines	Jenny Hagy	Steph Sines		
10-11							
11-12							

The Lab Is Closed When A Consultant Is Not On Duty.

running smoothly, that all software and hardware problems are noted, and that no important jobs are left undone. Figure 7.10 represents a duty-log sheet designed by the staff of the facility at Michigan Tech, a facility that depends on volunteer consultants for most of its daily operations support.

RECORDKEEPING SUGGESTION #5: Reservation Information

Most labs/classrooms that operate in academic settings must have flexible procedures for reserving computers: procedures that allow individual users to sign up for machines on a "walk-in" basis, and procedures that allow a teacher to reserve the entire roomful of machines for a biweekly class meeting. The forms that labs/classrooms use for this purpose vary, of course, with facility size, instructional goals, and demand. Figure 7.11 shows one form that allows for flexible reservations on behalf of both individuals and classes.

RECORDKEEPING SUGGESTION #6: Expendable Supplies Information

Keeping track of existing supplies and ordering new supplies for a computer-supported writing lab/classroom is no small task. Depending on the level of facility use, the time of the year, and the motivation of students, expendable supplies like paper, printer ribbons and thimbles, disks, and screen cleaner can disappear overnight. To make sure that lab/classroom operations are not interrupted because of a lack of basic supplies, most facilities keep close tabs on existing levels of supplies. Figure 7.12 represents a form that one computer-supported writing lab/classroom uses for such a task.

Figure 7.10: Duty-Log Sheet

CONSULTANT'S DUTY LOG			
DATE	NAME	TASKS COMPLETED	COMMENTS AND PROBLEMS

Figure 7.11: Reservations Sheet

RESERVATIONS SIGN-UP

DATE _____   HOUR _____

IBM   IBM

A _____   M _____

B _____   N _____

C _____   O _____

D _____   P _____

E _____   Q _____

F _____   R _____

G _____   S _____

H _____   T _____

I _____   U _____

J _____   V _____

K _____   W _____

L _____   X _____

Macintosh   Macintosh

A _____   B _____

Figure 7.12: Supplies Form

WEEKLY SUPPLY FORM

DATE:_____

Item	Description	Optimal Level	On-Hand	Order
Paper				
	8 x 14 regular perf.	30		
	11 x 14 wide perf.	5		
	8 x 11 bond perf.	5		
Ribbons				
	NEC mylar	10		
	NEC nylon	25		
	IBM Quietwriter	5		
	Macintosh	5		
Disks				
	Macintosh ss/dd	30		
	IBM	30		
Thimbles				
	NEC Courier-12	5		
Cleaning Supplies				
	Screen Cleaner	2		
	409	2		
	Garbage Bags	10		
Other				

RECORDKEEPING SUGGESTION #7: Security Records

Depending on their location and the nature of the student/ faculty populations they serve, some labs/classrooms find it necessary to keep regular records on the equipment they have available at any given time. The MTU facility that created the form represented in Figure 7.13, for instance, asked the consultant on duty during the last shift of each day to check off the presence of all available equipment. Such a procedure can deter thefts and help administrators pinpoint the time that equipment becomes missing in action.

RECORDKEEPING SUGGESTION #8: Maintenance and Repair

Computer-supported writing facilities of all sizes depend on regular machine maintenance and repair to assure that their operations run smoothly and without long-term interruptions. Unfortunately, keeping track of such maintenance and repair is not a simple task: equipment failures and problems must be logged and described in some systematic fashion, maintenance and repair visits must be recorded, continuing problems must be noted, and equipment removed for repair or maintenance must be tracked. Without proper recordkeeping systems, important information can get lost, forgotten, or ignored. Figures 7.14 and 7.15 represent two forms that might be useful in keeping track of maintenance and repair. Figure 7.14 represents a sample equipment-problem form on which lab/classroom staff members can systematically log any equipment failures or difficulties. Figure 7.15 represents a sample follow-up form on which the subsequent treatment of such problems is recorded by consultants or computer technicians.

RECORDKEEPING SUGGESTION #9: Hardware / Software Evaluations

Given the explosive nature of the computer industry and the unpredictable lifetime of software and hardware, most labs/

Figure 7.13: Equipment Check-Off Form

DATE:_____   CONSULTANT/STAFF:_____

Procedure	Observations/Notes	Check
1. Count Machines		
2. Count systems disks		
3. Turn off network		
4. Turn off printers		
5. Turn off stereo		
6. Unplug coffee pot		
7. Lock up software		
8. Lock door		
9. Arm alarm system		

Figure 7.14: Equipment Problem Log

(EQUIPMENT PROBLEM LOG)

DATE: _____   NETWORK: (**mono**) (**color**)

CONSULTANT: _____

MACHINE(S): _____
                   _____
                   _____

Description of Problem   (include complete messages,
                              application being used, etc.)

DURATION OF PROBLEM: _____

IDEAS: _____
         _____
         _____

Figure 7.15: Follow-up Form

FOLLOW-UP FORM

DATE:_____ CONSULTANT:_____
TIME: _____ TIME ON TASK: _____

Problem Diagnosis:

Software Modifications:

Hardware Modifications:

Duration of Fix: (Temporary)   (Permanent)

Recommendations:

classrooms are involved in a continuing cycle of evaluation, improvement, and purchase. This ongoing activity has to be documented if it is to be systematic and valuable to the administrators of such facilities.

Several recordkeeping forms may prove useful for this evaluation effort. Hardware/software evaluation forms, as represented in Figures 7.16 and 7.17, for instance, allow the staff of a lab/classroom to keep records of research done on particular software packages and brands of hardware. When purchasing decisions need to be made, these evaluation forms make ideal references. In addition, purchase/update forms allow lab/ classroom administrators to keep a historical record of a particular piece of software or hardware. As Figure 7.18 indicates, a purchase/update form for a software package might indicate when the package was purchased, when it was upgraded, or when the lab/classroom staff discontinued its use. purchase/update forms for hardware might include date of purchase, maintenance or repair records, upgrades or peripheral additions, serial numbers, and unsolved problems of an intermittent nature.

RECORDKEEPING SUGGESTION #10: Documentation

The staffs of most computer-supported writing facilities operating in academic settings find it necessary to rewrite the software and hardware documentation that originally comes with products purchased for instructional use. Such "factory-packed" documentation is often incomplete, generally ill suited for the instructional level of lab/classroom users, or simply incomprehensible to non-expert users of any age. If documentation writing is an activity that a lab/classroom staff does frequently to keep up with changing hardware and software, and newly purchased products, then some form of recordkeeping form may be helpful. The form shown in Figure 7.19 allows staff members to keep track of several valuable pieces of information in connection with documents: who wrote the latest revision of a document; when was each revision of a

Figure 7.16: Hardware Evaluation Form

HARDWARE EVALUATION FORM

Description:

Strengths:

Weaknesses:

Compatibility:

Comments/Recommendations:

| buy | consider | don't buy |

Figure 7.17: Software Evaluation Form

SOFTWARE EVALUATION FORM

Purpose/Description:

Strengths:

Weaknesses:

Comments/Recommendations:

| buy | consider | don't buy |

Figure 7.18: Purchase Update Form

PURCHASE/UPDATE FORM

Name of Package: _____
Purchase Date: _____ **Purchase Price:** _____
Company: _____
_____
_____

Status Change:

UPGRADE
    Date: _____ **Price:** _____
    Comments: _____
_____
_____

UPGRADE
    Date: _____ **Price:** _____
    Comments: _____
_____
_____

UPGRADE
    Date: _____ **Price:** _____
    Comments: _____
_____
_____

DISCONTINUE
    Date: _____ **Substitute:** _____
    Comments: _____
_____

Figure 7.19: Documentation Update Form

DOCUMENTATION UPDATE

Document: _____

Purpose: _____
           _____
           _____

Audience: _____

Disk/File: _____

Documentation Update:

   Author: _____   Date: _____

   Comments: _____
             _____
             _____

Documentation Update:

   Author: _____   Date: _____

   Comments: _____
             _____
             _____

document completed; where (on what disk and in what file) is the document stored; and what problems, suggestions, or limitations should be considered when a specific document is being prepared.

Although the range and number of recordkeeping forms in the preceding list, and the work they represent in terms of collecting and recording data, is enough to daunt even the most energetic lab administrator or staff member, our listing is necessarily incomplete. Each computer-supported writing facility, depending on its particular instructional goals and constraints, will need different kinds of recordkeeping forms. College administrators, content-area supervisors, deans, and department heads often have their own agenda for computer-supported writing labs and may need or request different kinds of recordkeeping information. Lab staff, lab faculty, and lab administrators may also require different kinds of data. Given this caution, it might be wise to think about "when is enough enough?" When does a facility's recordkeeping activities begin to limit instruction by diverting the time and energy of the staff? The answer to these questions can be answered only in light of each facility's instructional and operational goals. When recordkeeping activities in a facility begin to limit the staff's ability to achieve the instructional and operational goals that drive a lab/classroom, then the facility's administrator must consider alternatives.

Chapter Eight

Problems and Possibilities in a Computer-Supported Writing Facility

Given the essentially experimental nature of computer-supported writing facilities, they are bound to present both new problems and new possibilities to the established writing programs that spawn them. Fortunately, it is just such challenges which serve to keep alive and vibrant a department, a content-area, or a profession. The introduction of computers into our profession on a national level and into specific English programs on a local level has required faculty and administrators to join together and engage in some creative problem solving that focuses on the teaching of language arts. This increased attention to teaching, the formation of new alliances and communities among English teachers and administrators, and the rethinking and "re-vision" of traditional instructional methods and approaches can only help to promote new growth, encourage new ways of solving long-standing problems, and inspire new efforts on the part of educators at all levels.

The intellectual growth that occurs in the face of such upheaval, although exciting, can at the same time be disturbing. This chapter begins by outlining some of the problems that a computer-supported writing facility may introduce into an English program or department. Specifically, this chapter explores problems of personnel, access, and resource allocation in connection with computer-supported writing facilities. After sketching the broad outlines of these challenges, the chapter also suggests some of the advantages that may accrue to departments or programs that establish computer-supported writing facilities. In particular, it focuses on the increased level of collaborative activity that occurs around computers and within computer-supported facilities, the increased level of curricular involvement often inspired by the integration of computer support, and the increased interest in classroom research that results from introducing computers into English courses.

Problems in Paradise: The Downside of Computer-Support for English Composition Programs

Recent studies of organizations, businesses, and institutions that have introduced computers into office settings identify three common problem areas associated with such a venture: personnel, access to technology, and resource allocation. Applying these findings, in a more specific sense, to computer-supported writing facilities in school environments can be helpful to faculty and administrators who need some indication of the problems and challenges that a new program of computer support might present for an English composition program. Certainly, faculty connected with computer-supported writing facilities can expect to grapple, at one time or another, with these same three problem areas. Each of these challenges is discussed in detail on the following pages.

CHALLENGE #1: Personnel

Perhaps the first and most evident challenge an English program will have to face in connection with computers involves people rather than machines. As with any problem involving professional personnel, such difficulties have several layers of complexity. First, of course, is the problem of finding competent English teachers to administer computer-supported writing facilities. But this initial difficulty is only the beginning. Not only must deans, department heads, and faculty committees be able to identify teachers who are willing to work with and specialize in the use of computers, but also they must learn how to support the work of these individuals and reward the efforts of such teachers in an equitable manner.

That these tasks may prove challenging within a department of English is of little wonder given the nature of our profession. Most English programs, as we know from first-hand experience, are still built on relatively traditional foundations. The great majority of teachers now working in English programs have been trained as classical humanists or literary scholars. Given this educational background, most of us are personally invested in the value of traditional literary pursuits, in the areas of teaching, scholarship, and publication. This background also determines how comfortable English teachers are with various instructional media. For most of us, the medium of choice is still print; books, journals, and papers are the currency of intellectual exchange, not computers, software, and technology. Such a value system necessarily influences all aspects of a department's infrastructure, including the granting of tenure and promotion, the selection of lower-level administrative personnel, and the assignment of desirable courses and student populations.

But although our profession is traditionally oriented in this sense, it is forward-looking in another. Administrators seldom find it difficult, even within the most traditional of departments, to identify at least one teacher within the English faculty who has an interest in computers and a certain level of competence in connection with their use. Indeed, it is becoming increasingly less common to find English teachers who lack familiarity with at least one word-processing package. Although not all of these teachers are willing to increase their computer involvement to the level of administering a computer-supported writing lab/classroom, it is fast becoming possible to find individuals who are eager to do so. These faculty members frequently have a vision of what computers can do to support the instruction currently underway within a program and, as a result, are willing to help plan, implement, and administer a computer-supported writing facility.

It is also true, however, that faculty members who accept the role of official, or even unofficial, computer specialists in an English department often find traditional values working against them. These teachers, for example, may accept the charge of administering a computer-supported writing facility only to discover that their technologically-based contributions are evaluated differently from their work in more traditional fields. In many colleges and universities, for example, the time a teacher spends planning, designing, and operating a successful lab/classroom, training students and teachers to use the facility effectively, or developing instructional software is undervalued or even ignored.

Fortunately, this situation is generally the result of inexperience rather than conscious prejudice on the part of a department's faculty. Because computer-supported writing facilities are new to our profession, few English departments can accurately gauge the labor needed to sustain the operation. Indeed, if a lab/classroom is operating successfully, much of this labor may be invisible to colleagues or departmental administrators.

To combat this situation, deans, departmental administrators, and tenure and promotion committees can learn to revise their thinking about professional contributions in light of the special challenges faced by English teachers/computer specialists. Among other considerations, for instance, departmental administrators can review and credit the time these faculty members spend in organizing and implementing computer-literacy programs; developing computer-assisted instruction and writing the documentation that accompanies it; supervising lab/classroom staff and student volunteers; working with facility budgets and ordering expendable supplies; reviewing software and hardware; coordinating lab tours, classes, and introductions; upgrading their own technical expertise; dealing with technical specialists and arranging maintenance schedules; and coordinating departmental computer efforts with school-wide or college-wide efforts. Once these contributions are identified, farsighted administrators can also be helpful in pointing out how such activities contribute to departmental goals and objectives within the framework of the larger educational institution and in determining an appropriate incentive program.

CHALLENGE #2: Access

The issue of access to technology is becoming increasingly central and increasingly political within educational settings. Critics describe a growing schism between those academic institutions that can afford to buy into the technological age and those that cannot, and between those students who can afford to buy computers and those who cannot. More specifically, English teachers' growing awareness of the power connected with computer-assisted language learning and language production assures continued concern with the topic of access, especially as it relates to computer-supported writing facilities. Most of the larger issues associated with access are manifested specifically in computer-supported labs/classrooms, and all have a bearing on the students and teachers associated with such facilities.

Nor are these issues easily resolved. In many cases, we simply lack sufficient information to make careful, informed,

and consistent decisions. One example of this dilemma involves the impact computers have on writers. Although investigators in our field generally agree that the use of computers
can affect individuals' attitudes toward writing, the processes
by which they compose and the texts that they produce, the
results of these investigations have been mixed at best. Our
profession still does not have a clear picture of whether these
effects are negative or positive in nature, whether they are
consistent for writers with varied learning styles or writing
experience, or whether they are affected by hardware/soft-
ware/site variables. Yet it is with this cloudy vision that we are
forced to operate at the present time. Using it, we must decide,
as a profession and as individual teachers, whether to provide
access for students who want to use computers in support of
their writing and language production activities and how this
task is best achieved.

Even if our profession were clearer about the complicated
issue of access to computer technology, our efforts would continue to be limited by economic realities.   Currently, few
colleges and universities can claim that all students have equal
access to computers for use in English composition. Some
schools, in fact, provide students access to computers for use in
mathematics and science applications but not in connection
with English composition activities. Often, English teachers
who are convinced of the computer's power as a tool for language production and who are willing to develop classes that
take advantage of technological support must also assume
responsibility for pressing access claims in the face of considerable odds.

Moreover, even when English teachers are convinced of the
advantages of computer-supported writing and they are successful in obtaining access to computers for composition courses,
they may find other access-related factors limiting to students.
Computer-support for writing at home, for instance, may in
reality be limited to those students from upper- and middle-
class families. A teacher may hesitate to tie lengthy writing
assignments to computers when only half the class can work

effectively on their drafting efforts after school hours. Similarly, teachers may observe that students who do have access to a computer and word-processing package at home have other advantages over their peers. These students may learn to use additional word-processing packages more quickly than neophyte computer users, may be more confident and less anxious about computer-supported writing than other students, and may be more willing or able to experiment with computer-supported writing than their less experienced counterparts. For some teachers, these disparities raise disturbing questions of equality in educational opportunity.

Finally, English teachers must also concern themselves with continuity and consistency in access. As we teach more and more students to become dependent on computers for language-production activities, we are obligated to provide more and larger computer-supported facilities. For instance, one English faculty at a small four-year college with limited computer resources recently fought for and won computer access for students in first-year English classes. The aim of the program was to provide each entering class a short-term program in computer literacy and word processing during the first year of college education, and then, in the second, third, and fourth years, to encourage computer use for more traditional applications in science and technical classes. To their dismay, the English faculty found the program too successful. By the end of the year, the same students who had complained about having to use a computer for their first English composition course had come to consider the faculty ethically bound to provide continuing, and indeed increased, support in second-year, third-year, and fourth-year writing classes. Computer use at the school went up over 300% in a single year, and the funding for additional equipment was nowhere to be found.

Similar pressures for access are just as evident on a smaller scale. Teachers now commonly share stories of students who blame incomplete writing assignments on power surges and equipment failures, who claim they must have access to computers to complete in-class essay examinations, or who claim that their computer-dependent composing strategies prevent them from thinking effectively in the absence of a keyboard.

Faculty also require access to computers, and the political nature of access decisions is just as evident when they concern teachers as when they concern students. Many English teachers, for instance, have become only too aware of the power that computer technology can lend teachers of writing—the power of access to information, of document storage and retrieval, of communication with other writers, of desktop publication and document design, of electronic paper exchanges, and of technologically-supported lesson presentations. As a result of the growing demand for computers as instructional-support tools, English departments have begun to redefine their stance on providing computer-access for teachers, paraprofessionals, staff members, and content-area administrators. Departments and schools may soon be faced with the obligation to provide all faculty members equal access to computers in support of their professional activities and to provide equal access to training programs that help faculty take advantage of this computer support.

In fulfilling this obligation, our profession will most certainly encounter a series of complicated and involved decisions. First, in most situations, comes a financial question: Who will pay for such access or such training? Equally thorny, however, are the following questions: Given the limited nature of most schools' computer facilities, how do we choose which faculty have priority to a computer-supported lab/classroom or to a computer designated for teacher-only use? Can colleges and universities require that individual teachers become computer literate themselves before their classes can make use of a computer-supported lab/classroom? If instructors teach computer-supported classes, do we have to provide them compatible computers and software with which to prepare their class materials or provide them access to secretarial staff trained on such equipment? Do teachers have priority over students in matters of computer access?

CHALLENGE #3: *Resource Allocation*

The problem of resource allocation faces any English program that decides to integrate computer support into existing instruction. Even English teachers and educators who have had extensive experience in planning, funding, or staffing traditional writing laboratories or reading/writing centers are staggered by the time, money, and energy that computer-supported operations absorb. Any administrator who has seen the evolution of a computer-supported lab/classroom can attest to the endless stream of resources that flow into such a facility. Thus, the task of carefully and realistically planning for the integration of a computer-supported lab/classroom becomes increasingly important for faculty and administrators who want to avoid the frustration of unexpected obstacles.

First, as we noted earlier in this chapter, computer labs/classrooms require personnel. Although previous sections of this book outline in more detail the various configurations of a lab staff, a department considering the possibility of adding extensive computer support to an existing English program can generally count on devoting the equivalent of one full-time faculty position to such an operation. Often, personnel commitments are split between full- and part-time staff members, who share the administrative burden of the facility and are supported by individuals (faculty, students, and staff) who are paid an hourly wage or who volunteer their time.

Such personnel commitments can cause immediate difficulties within a department. A faculty operating under a hiring freeze, for example, may face the choice of getting along with one fewer content-area teacher in order to allocate personnel resources to a computer-supported lab/classroom or to break up a full-time position into several part-time positions to answer a similar need. Indeed, given the relatively limited number of English teachers who are willing to specialize in computer support of English programs, even departments that enjoy a versatile faculty and strong budgetary support may be unable to fill traditional content-area obligations when the additional burden of a computer-supported writing facility is added to departmental responsibilities.

A second major challenge connected with resource allocation involves funding—both initial funding and funding on a continuing basis. As a rule, given the interest of granting agencies, computer companies, and private foundations in computer-supported educational efforts, the task of finding initial funding has generally proven to be the less difficult of the two fiscal dilemmas. Unfortunately, the fact that relatively "easy" money is available for the initial purchase of computers can, and has, exacerbated the problem of continuing funding.

Deans, department heads, principals, or teachers—finding themselves suddenly rich with a grant for the purchase of computer—are frequently tempted to buy machines and software without fully considering the problems involved in ongoing funding and often end up with a lab/classroom that fits neither their needs nor their expectations. Such situations cannot always be avoided by careful planning on the part of a seasoned administrator. Often, funds allocated for equipment purchase are discovered only at the end of a fiscal year and must be spent within a limited time frame. In such cases, unless farsighted faculty committees have already agreed on the instructional and operational goals for a computer-supported facility and identified the specific hardware and software capabilities implied by these goals, the resulting choices will be hit or miss.

In similarly problematic situations, the initial funding for a computer-supported English composition facility includes only monies allocated for computer equipment. A department may find itself, in such cases, scouring the cafeteria for extra tables and chairs on which to put the machines and robbing the departmental budget for money to purchase software. Nor do such scenarios improve as these facilities age: computer-supported writing facilities are expensive to maintain on a continuing basis. Elsewhere in this book, we have identified more systematically the continuing expenses a department can expect to incur: the purchase of ergonomically sound furniture, expendable supplies (paper, printer ribbons, printer wheels, toner cartridges, and disks), software purchases and updates, hardware maintenance and repair, personnel costs, equipment replacement, cleaning supplies—the list goes on and on. In fact, one Midwestern university president has described computers as a "black hole" for funds.

A good portion of this money-drain is attributable to the explosive and exciting nature of the computer industry itself. Experts now estimate that computer companies operate on a marketing cycle of five years or less. Thus, an academic consumer—a college, computer-supported writing lab/classroom, or a department—can expect any given computer, and its various parts, to be maintained by the company that produced it for a period of five years or less. After this time, a new product and line, which may or may not be immediately compatible with the older product, will be out. Upgrading older equipment, consumers soon learn, may be more expensive than buying the new equipment itself.

Computers themselves, however, represent only a portion of the money drain: the rising cost of insurance, the increasing need for security systems to protect computer facilities, and the high cost of sophisticated repair and maintenance all contribute to the costs associated with a computer-supported writing lab/classroom; the list can go on far too long. For most English departments, these expenses—which are not only new, but also often underestimated—wreak havoc on already overloaded budgets. Without careful and realistic planning, departments that have already committed initial funding to a computer-supported facility find themselves faced with a series of "no win" decisions: more library books or computer support, yearly professional journal subscriptions or computer support, and faculty travel funds or computer support.

In the long run, then, it seems clear that schools or departments planning a computer-supported writing facility must have institutional backing if they hope to succeed in the face of these challenges. Such support may be financial (a continuing budget, a portion of tuition funds, permission to assess a users' fee), administrative (personnel, scheduling, incentives), or technical (programming, repair, maintenance), but the existence of such support is crucial. Without help, few departments can bear the burden of expensive facilities, even if such facilities are demonstrably successful in an instructional sense. Adhering to a careful program of facility planning, as we suggested in the first three chapters of this book, can help establish support and eliminate many of the surprises associated with continuing funding.

The Potential of Computers: Taking Advantage of Technology

Although the advice in the preceding sections suggests a rather cautious fiscal approach, computerized labs/classrooms are becoming increasingly popular, and there are good reasons for this fact. Despite the problems associated with personnel, access, and resource allocation, computer-supported facilities can encourage an exciting spirit of intellectual community among teachers and students; increase faculty involvement with existing English curricula; and inspire creative and energetic new research efforts that serve the profession within a larger context.

BENEFIT #1: Increased Collaboration

Certainly a delightful benefit of establishing a computer-supported writing facility is the increased collaborative activity that results on the part of both faculty and students. Faculty are often the first to experience this advantage as they learn to use computers for their own work. Because computer technology is still new to the lives of most English teachers, the machines seldom fail to encourage a sense of group curiosity, playfulness, and experimentation. When several computers are placed together in a single writing facility, they begin to act as magnets, drawing faculty together in one place that is devoted exclusively to the effort of writing, or talking about writing, or exchanging ideas about writing and language. In working within such a computer facility, a faculty often discovers a sense of community that comes to be valued as a regular part of departmental life.

Most English teachers, of course, are long-time advocates of the kind of collaborative writing activities that are fostered within a computer-supported writing facility and have set up their traditional classrooms to encourage these activities among their students. These teachers know how important it is for writers to interact and exchange information at all stages of their writing process and thus have always encouraged students to try a range of cooperative composing strategies. For these English teachers, computer-supported writing labs/classrooms fit neatly and easily into a well-established conceptual framework. In fact, facilities that offer computer support for writing allow these teachers to encourage collaborative energy among their students and bring language groups together in productive new ways.

Because these rooms are designed for writers, students are generally quick to see them as gathering places for serious work on composition. But, because the computer "belongs" to the younger generation, students also frequently come to feel a proprietary interest in these "writing places" and work to shape them to their own purposes. In many labs/classrooms, for instance, students who have previous computer experience volunteer to serve as consultants. Although these young experts revel in their mastery over technology, they are also gaining experience in teaching writers about writing and sharing ideas about writing strategies and composing efforts with their peers. The process of discovering how to use computer technology to support their writing activities frequently acts as the cement for such collaborative communities. Students, even when not led by their instructors, feel challenged to play with computers, to discover how to send on-line messages to members of their group, to teach each other how to handle common document problems, and to experiment together with graphics and spelling software.

In collaboratively-based writing labs, these practical strategies for computer use often grow out of student suggestions and experimentation. Students discover, for instance, that they can type revision suggestions right into an individual's draft and differentiate their own comments from the author's text by hitting the "Caps Lock" key. Left to their own devices, students find out how to take advantage of color, blinking characters, and other techniques of highlighting on the computer screen to call attention to their revision advice.

In writing-intensive computer labs/classrooms that support faculty as well as student writers, students frequently receive strong doses of collaborative modeling, observing the effects of cooperative writing in the most immediate sense. They see faculty working together to solve rhetorical problems and note the advantages of combining the writing processes and strategies of several creative minds. These same students generally see that collaboration comes naturally when writers work in close quarters and that technology can facilitate such efforts.

In fact, the communities fostered within computer-supported writing labs/classrooms frequently cross traditional social and academic boundaries. When these facilities bring teachers and students together as writers in one space, both groups benefit from observing the other at work. Students have the opportunity to learn that teachers agonize over words, that they struggle with organization, word choice, and arrangement. At the same time, teachers can observe their students, watching the effects of specific course assignments and the effort that students put into communication problems.

The blurring of traditional social boundaries in computer-supported writing "spaces" has additional benefits as well. Students who know more about computers than instructors often become the "teachers" and demonstrate formatting tricks, printer commands, and software functions. Faculty, who may have limited knowledge of computers, learn once again what it is like to be faced with communication problems that involve unfamiliar and potentially threatening elements.

BENEFIT #2: Increased Curricular Engagement

A second benefit of integrating computer support into an existing English composition program grows out of the necessity of curricular adjustment. Such involvement may start with the planning of a lab/classroom, but it generally continues and builds as the facility begins operating and faculty members become more sophisticated about their use of technology in classroom settings.

If a faculty does a careful job of planning for a computer-supported writing facility, curricular issues are raised early in the process of establishing a lab/classroom and shape all subsequent design decisions made in connection with the lab. In many situations, the planning of a computer facility acts as the impetus for curricular discussions and reconceptualizations. Faculty, who when left to their own devices seldom find time to discuss curricular issues with their colleagues, are encouraged to do so when computers become a focus for departmental efforts and they are asked to participate in computer-literacy programs or teach computer-supported writing classes.

Generally, although not always, the upshot of these discussions is a pleasant surprise. Most English teachers, when pressed to identify their assumptions about writing and the teaching of writing, agree on broad educational planks: the complexly recursive nature of most writing tasks; the importance of writing processes as well as products; the crucial benefits of teacher and peer feedback in a process-based writing classroom; and the centrality of considerations such as audience, rhetorical setting, and purpose. When these concepts are raised in discussions of computer support for an English program, a faculty often comes to an improved collective understanding of larger questions about the shape and direction of a writing program as a whole.

This increased level of curricular involvement seldom wanes once a computer facility has been established. Indeed, it often builds as more teachers begin to integrate computer use into their classes. Although most teachers find it initially fruitful to embrace playfulness and experimentation with computers as they learn along with their students to master the new technology, they also quickly discover that some strategies work consistently well in computer-supported classes while others frequently fall flat. Often the explanation for such experiences involves curricular integration and integrity: teachers discover that computer use that is related organically to a subject matter generally succeeds, but computer use that is "tacked on" to a content area generally fails. The result of these discoveries, when coupled with a faculty's growing collective sophistication with computers, contribute to a heightened sense of curricular awareness on the part of a faculty.

As Chapter Five explains, teachers who are serious about integrating computers into their classes in an effective and organic way are forced to reexamine, and sometimes to discover for the first time, their own assumptions about writing and the teaching of writing. In fact, the very nature of a computer-supported classroom, because it is different in focus and arrangement from a traditional classroom, requires teachers to alter their traditional teaching activities, assignments, and presentations. These modifications, in turn, lead to curricular revision at the most basic level.

BENEFIT #3: Increased Research Activity

Because computer-supported writing facilities change the nature and teaching of writing dramatically, it is not surprising that they also encourage teachers to engage in research and observation projects that inform and shape the instruction going on in a department. Included in these efforts may be projects aimed at identifying the effects of computers on composing processes, collaborative writing efforts, and written products; at exploring issues connected with computer ethics, computer-assisted instruction, and computer apprehension; and at addressing such topics as computer-assisted grading, computer literacy, and computer access.

The impetus behind such research on computer-supported writing is not difficult to understand. Teachers who offer lab-based writing classes for the first time necessarily become acutely aware of the subtle ways in which computers affect students' composing processes, both positively and negatively. Although research on computers is becoming increasingly available, many of the questions that teachers formulate as natural by-products of their own instructional efforts remain unanswered. In the best situations, departmental infrastructures offer these teachers support while they try to answer questions for themselves. The value of these research efforts, growing as they do out of classroom experience, is that they inform not only an instructor's teaching and that of his or her immediate colleagues but that they also enrich the profession as a whole.

It is also important to note that computer-supported writing facilities provide a particular set of benefits to teachers/researchers that are not available in traditional classroom settings. First, for instance, computer-supported writing facilities are uniquely suited to qualitative research. These sites commonly serve as gathering places for student writers who are solving writing problems outside a structured classroom setting, thus providing teachers/researchers with the opportunity for observation less constrained by particular instructional agendas. Second, because of the equipment these sites contain, they frequently provide investigators with an electronic means of observing and recording data.

Computer-supported writing labs/classrooms also offer teachers/researchers the challenge of a new research frontier, one that remains essentially unexplored by the members of previous generations. For teachers, who may be hesitant to embark on research projects that have a long history of built-in political constraints, this aspect can be alluring. Teachers/researchers can use lab/classroom studies to explore such diverse issues as the role of hard copy in the writing process, the advantages computers offer in helping students to write from primary sources, the nature and characteristics of electronically-produced teacher comments and peer feedback, and the potential and limitations of using computers to produce comments on style, grammar, usage, and language in student compositions.

Labs/classrooms can also serve as testing sites for new and exciting interdisciplinary research. In these facilities, English composition teachers can replicate, modify, or add to the investigatory work done in other fields and apply the results directly to the teaching of writing in a technologically-supported environment. Writing teachers can, for instance, turn to related research on ergonomics and the physical layout of computer labs to inform their use of computers in writing centers and classrooms. Ergonomic studies could help teachers decide, among other things, whether they should change the lighting in writing centers when computers are added, how computers should be arranged to minimize keyboard and printer noise for writers, how computer screens and copy stands should be tilted to help writers avoid eye strain, or how specific kinds of chairs could help reduce muscular-skeletal fatigue for writers during long drafting sessions.

In other interdisciplinary projects, psychology-based studies carried out in computer-supported writing facilities could help teachers investigate how or if computers affect short- and long-term memory as it is used in the writing process and reading and writing apprehension. Such studies might also explore how or why some writers are afraid to use computers or what psychological constraints are involved when authors use computers as writing tools. In addition, hemispheric studies of brain function might help English composition teachers discover whether some writing assignments might be better handled on the computers than others; whether certain fonts and colors on computer screens are more readable or more effective than others; and how gender, hemispheric asymmetry, and computer-assisted writing all fit together.

Chapter Nine

Making Connections

Previous chapters in this book have been concerned with designing and operating computer-supported writing labs/ classrooms within particular educational settings. As we have noted, each site bears the stamp of its immediate environment: the English program, faculty, and students the facility supports; the constraints under which it has been established; and the assumptions and goals that shape its instruction and operation. However, in at least one important sense, a successful lab/classroom cannot be simply local in its conception or operation. To grow more sophisticated in approach, to share stories of success and failure within similar facilities, and to build on the discoveries that other English teachers and educators have made, staff members must reach out and make connections within a larger professional context.

In fact, for some teachers associated with designing, building, and operating a computer-supported writing lab, the job only begins when the lab is opened and supporting instruction. It is often at this time that teachers recognize a crucial need to share their work and their expertise with colleagues in order to better understand the tasks and issues that teachers must wrestle with. Of course, these connections can be made at any number of levels. Some educators feel responsible for discussing their experiences and decisions with other colleagues in their own English departments; others want to make sense of their experience in a broader way, perhaps by discussing the general advantages and disadvantages of labs/classrooms to large groups of teachers at professional conferences; still others hope to write about what they have learned while attempting to integrate computer support into their own departments and distribute these materials to colleagues they may never meet in person.

This chapter is directed toward teachers, both users and administrators of computer-supported labs/classrooms, who can see the advantages of sharing their experiences with colleagues and making connections with other teachers involved in similar educational ventures. We suggest three forums for faculty who wish to talk about their particular lab/classroom set-ups to other English professionals: sharing experiences with groups of English teachers and educators, making direct connections with other facilities currently in operation, and writing about experiences in professional publications.

SUGGESTION #1: Sharing Experiences With Other Teachers

One of the most effective ways of getting other teachers interested in computer-support for English programs or computer-supported writing labs/classrooms is to undertake a series of local discussions on the topic. Teachers who have had a hand in planning, operating, or teaching in such a facility often find it helpful sharing experiences and thoughts with other colleagues in their own English department, with teachers in other disciplines who teach writing-intensive courses, and with English faculty from other institutions. Often these presentations are given at faculty meetings held in the teacher's department, shared in college- or university-wide colloquia, shown as a part of regional curriculum workshops, given as papers at professional conventions, or prepared as a component of summer writing projects.

In fact, the only problem with giving presentations of this kind is that they are *so* popular. Composition teachers of all sorts, working at all levels, are hungry for lessons in how to use computers in a way that is both theoretically and practically sound. Once a teacher shares stories of a successful lab/classroom with colleagues, the computer-user grapevine is activated, and requests begin to pile up.

To be effective, a presentation about a particular computer-supported writing facility requires practice, advanced planning, and organization. The list below provides several things to think about during the planning of a presentation:

Philosophy and Background: Think of beginning presentations about your computer-supported English program or lab/classroom by letting the audience in on important background information. Sketch, briefly but completely, the educational assumptions and goals that originally formed the impetus for your program or facility. This information then becomes the basis on which the audience can evaluate and understand the efforts that have shaped and continue to direct your work with computers or the way in which you have designed, established, and operated your computer-supported writing facility.

The Site: If you are talking about an existing computer-supported lab/classroom, let your audience see the facility for themselves. If possible, hold the presentation within the lab/

classroom itself so that the audience can see the way in which machines are arranged; note the ways in which software, reference materials, and student work is stored; identify the activities that frequently go on in the room; and even get a sense of the facility's ambience with students and faculty working in it. If such an on-site visit is impossible, consider compiling a slide presentation or a video-taped tour of the facility to illustrate these components.

Documentation: Before the presentation, collect or write descriptive documentation for your computer-assisted writing center. Individuals who are planning their own facility or who want to improve an existing facility will frequently ask for such materials. As part of this documentation, think about including a brief description of the facility and its purpose; a list of the facility's major instructional and operational goals; examples of the writing activities the facility supports; faculty and student comments about the facility; lists of, and specifications for, the software and hardware available in the facility; lists of the "lessons" you have learned about establishing computer support in your English program; and diagrams of the room layout or equipment configurations that characterize the facility. In addition, provide the name and address of a contact person at your site that interested parties can write or call for further information.

Questions: Save plenty of time for questions about the computer-supported writing program and lab/classroom. During the first few presentations you give, record the queries and use them to shape your next presentation. Some teachers prepare answers for a list of "frequently asked" questions about their facility and distribute them along with other documentation.

In planning a presentation on a computer-supported writing facility, English composition teachers may want to think of several audiences who would find the information applicable and pertinent. Frequently, faculty members who talk about their computer-supported writing lab/classroom to an audience of local teachers will find it helpful to modify their presentation for a broader group of English educators. Professional conferences at the regional and national level are devoting increasing amounts of program time and exhibit space to teachers who are interested in computer-assisted writing instruction. Because these conferences attract a large number of teachers, teacher educators, and administrators, they are perfect places to talk about how to establish and operate computer-supported writing labs/classrooms for existing English composition programs.

Among the larger gatherings that encourage an exchange of information on computer-assisted language instruction are the annual meetings of the National Council of Teachers of English (NCTE), the Conference on College Composition and Communication (CCCC), the National Educational Computing Conference (NECC), and the International Reading Association (IRA). A host of other regional, national, and international conferences also provide forums for teachers who want to share information about computer support for writing programs. They include meetings such as Microcomputers and the Learning Process (Clarkson College), Computers and Writing, Microcomputers and Basic Skills in College (City University of New York), Computers and the Humanities, Writing for the Computer Industry, and the International Conference on Computers in the Humanities (ICCH). Most of these gatherings are announced well ahead of time in computer-focused professional journals for English educators (see the listing that follows under SUGGESTION #3) and accept papers, presentations, or workshops that focus on computer-support for work in the Humanities.

SUGGESTION #2: Making Connections with Other Programs

One of the most satisfying ways of sharing information about a particular computer-supported writing program or lab/classroom involves direct exchanges of information with other colleagues in similar situations. For some English teachers, this approach may involve looking only as far as a nearby college or university—any place where colleagues are working actively with computer support for English composition programs.

Other teachers, however, may have to look harder and farther for colleagues who are integrating computers into an existing English program. Fortunately, our profession is beginning to identify and foster networks of teachers who are struggling with problems of computer integration within English/language arts studies. Many of these networks and organizations publish newsletters and information sheets that can help teachers identify colleagues engaged in similar projects. Some of the larger organizations are listed below. Ask English teachers who use computers in your own school or department for organizations operating on a local level.

Minnesota Educational Computing Consortium (MECC)
3490 Lexington Ave.
St. Paul, MN 55126

National Council of Teachers of English
Instructional Technology Committee
1111 Kenyon Rd.
Urbana, IL 61801

Conference on College Composition and
Communication
Committee on Computers
National Council of Teachers of English
1111 Kenyon Rd.
Urbana, IL 61801

When corresponding with these networking organizations, both on the national and local levels, it is best to include a self-addressed and stamped envelope for replies. Many of these groups operate on a lean budget that allows little room for unplanned mailing expenses.

It is also important to note that these networks are valuable because the people within them are willing to share, openly and honestly, their expertise and experience. The teachers who belong to them have similar interests and support each other's efforts to incorporate computers into writing classrooms and programs. These teachers keep each other informed about new technological developments in computer hardware and software; new methodological developments in writing-intensive, computer-assisted learning situations; and new theoretical, philosophical, and ethical concerns that the introduction of computers may inspire.

SUGGESTION #3: *Writing in Professional Publications*

With leaner budgets and increasing travel costs, it is not always possible to talk in person with other teachers about computer-supported English composition programs. Articles and descriptions in professional journals provide one way of getting around this problem by allowing you to distribute information about facilities to larger audiences. Articles can serve not only to describe the purpose and structure of your facility, but also to report empirical evidence of the program's effectiveness, to suggest broad guidelines for setting up similar facilities, and to share solutions to the common problems that lab/classroom teachers face. Some of the computer-focused professional journals that have published articles related to computer-supported writing programs are included in the following list:

Collegiate Microcomputer
Brian Winkel, Editor
Rose-Hulman Institute of Technology
Terre Haute, IN 47803

Computers and the Humanities
Joseph Raben, Editor
Paradigm Press, Inc.
Osprey, FL 33559

Computers and Composition
Gail E. Hawisher, Editor
Department of English
Purdue University
West Lafayette, IN 47907
                    or
Cynthia L. Selfe, Editor
Humanities Department
Michigan Technological University
Houghton, MI 49931

The Computer-Assisted Composition Journal
Lynn Veach Sadler and Wendy Tibbetts Greene, Editors
Methodist College
Fayetteville, NC 28301-1499

Look over back copies of these publications and request editorial information before writing or submitting an article about your computer-supported writing lab/classroom or program; each publication has specific guidelines for submissions.

Appendix

MICHIGAN TECHNOLOGICAL UNIVERSITY
INTERDEPARTMENTAL MEMORANDUM

TO: All Humanities Teachers
DATE: September 12, 1987
FROM: C. Selfe
RE: Center for Computer-Assisted Language Instruction (CCLI)

The CCLI is open and ready for business this term. You do not need to use the computers yourself in order to let your students profit from the CCLI. We can support your writing-intensive classes in a number of ways:

* by providing your students instruction on, and continuing help with, our word-processing program (Volkswriter III), spelling checkers, style analyzers, graphics programs, project-management programs, and chart-and-graph programs;

* by providing your students access to writing consultants who can help them with writing problems and assignments;

* by providing a computer-supported writing classroom in which you can hold classes and a computer-trained teaching assistant to help you with these classes;

* by storing your class handouts, tests, and assignments on our computers so that your students can have access to them; and

* by providing large-group introductions to our lab.

If you want to use the lab, please contact me or Dickie Selfe (call 7-2447 or leave a note in our mailboxes in WAHC 103). We will help in any way we can to tailor the CCLI services to your needs.

PLEASE ANNOUNCE TO YOUR STUDENTS that *any* student enrolled in a Humanities course may sign up to use the lab (HU011). Send interested students to Carol Johnson (WAHC 103) for an add slip, and then to the lab itself (WAHC 113) for instruction. HU011 carries with it a $20.00 lab fee per class.

Suggestions for Computer-Intensive Courses

* Have your handouts typed on a floppy disk, and put it on reserve in the lab for your students. Then the department secretaries won't have to run off handouts; students can read them on the computer screen (a paperless classroom) or print out hard copies as needed.

* Put certain writing activities on a floppy disk, and use it for those class meetings that you hold in the lab. In one class period, for example, you might plan to have students rewrite a memorandum in small groups. Put the memo on your floppy disk, schedule the class meeting for the lab, and let students rewrite on the computers.

* Put past quizzes, tests, and student papers on an floppy disk, and keep it on reserve in the lab so students can have access to valuable study/writing guides for your class.

* Put current tests on a floppy disk and have students meet in the lab to take tests.

* Have students write their journals on the computer. Put sample entries (labeled "successful" and/ or "not-so-successful") on an floppy disk, and put it on reserve in the lab.

* Set up a dialogue or letter floppy disk on which students record their questions about your class and write you letters, and keep it on reserve in the lab. Once a week, you can read these questions and letters and respond to them on a computer. Some teachers might want to put their responses on individual students' disks; others might want to respond on a public disk so that all students in the class can benefit from each other's questions.

* Ask your students to keep their disks in the lab so that you can leave on-line messages. Be sure to negotiate "privacy" guidelines with your class before you do this. Students may not want you to have access to disks that contain their rough drafts. They may also want to have separate disks for private and public material.

* Schedule one class period in the first or second week during which we can introduce your entire class to

the word-processing software. Schedule a half-hour session in which you meet with us to discuss alternative ways of using computers in your class. In the coming budget and materials crunch, the lab can supply a number of inexpensive alternatives to the daily handout and hard-copy editing we often use in class. See us for specifics.

The Center for Computer-Assisted Language Instruction is now prepared to offer the following programs for your use and your students'. Our consultants will provide individualized instruction for each software package.

Word-Processing Programs

VOLKSWRITER III: An easy-to-learn program for students. VXIII has a built-in spelling checker with a 170,000 word dictionary and a document formatter.

THE FINAL WORD: A powerful program that meets professional needs. Does a number of document-design tricks including automatic indexing, footnoting, and section numbering.

NOTA BENE: The MLA recommends this one for scholars in our field. Has some useful bibliographic and footnoting features. A bit hard to learn for beginners, but advocates claim it's worth the effort.

MACWRITE: Simple and seductive, yet a moderately powerful word-processing program.

MICROSOFT WORD: Some say this is more powerful than MacWrite and easier to use.

Writing Aids

MICROSPELL: A moderately fast spelling checker with a dictionary of 60,000 words—provides correctly spelled guesses for your misspelled words.

ASPEN PROOFREADER: A spelling checker with a 20,000 word dictionary—fairly slow.

HAYDEN SPELLER: A spelling checker that claims to cover 97% of the most frequently used words in English. 20,000 word dictionary.

GRAMMATIK: A style analyzer that locates some simple grammatical errors and gives statistics on a text's average sentence length, word count, "to be" verbs, and prepositions.

WORDSWORK: A process-based program designed to help students with papers that have a narrative component. Reviews critical concepts connected with narratives for students. Provides practice exercises on these concepts and helps students brainstorm, plan, and focus narratives through a series of journal writes.

INVENTION PROGRAMS: A series of three rhetorically-based programs designed by Hugh Burns that help writers with invention in their writing efforts. Includes one set of invention prompts based on Aristotle's topoi; one based on Burke's dramatistic pentad; and one based on Pike, Becker, and Young's tagmemic matrix.

Document-Design Aids

CLICKART: A "scrapbook" of dandy little pictures that you can "paste" into documents at appropriate places.

MACDRAW: A program for creating structured graphics: flowcharts, architectural drawings, forms, presentations graphics, etc.

MACPAINT: An art program that allows you to draw freeform and cut and paste; create geometric designs; make presentation graphics; and copy on-screen forms. Makes great overheads with large print.

MICROSOFT CHART: A business graphics program that helps you produce a wide range of charts, graphs, and data presentations. Makes super overheads.

READY SET GO: An interactive program that assists you in setting up and laying out a complete page layout (newspapers, journals, magazines).

MACPUBLISH: An electronic publishing aid that includes a word-processing program. Allows you to design, edit, and print multicolumn texts and illustrations; choose fonts and point sizes; and "manipulate page geography" to create dummy layouts.

Special Communication Aids

TYPING TUTOR: A dynamite tutorial program for those who aren't keyboard experts. Includes traditional instruction, practice, and exercises at various levels of difficulty, and TYPING INVADERS—a game modeled on the popular SPACE INVADERS—that teaches typing skills.

READING-LEVEL ANALYSIS: A program that analyzes the readability level of any text using a variety of indices including Dale-Chall, Fog, Flesch, Fry, Smog, Wheeler-Smith, and Spache. Can be used to show students just how limited such indices can be.

PC FILE III: A powerful database program that helps you keep track of subscription lists, reports, price lists, telephone numbers, addresses, inventories, personnel, etc. Helps you create mailing labels and sort them by zip code, alphabetical order, or any other characteristic.

Index

budgetary support, 123
cleaning supplies, 125
computer vendors' marketing cycle, 125
equipment, 124-125
expendable supplies, 124
financial support, 125
fiscal approach, 126
funding, initial/continuing, 124-125
furniture, ergonomically-sound, 124
institutional backing, 125
insurance, 125
maintenance and repair, 124-125
personnel, 123-124
programming (as support), 125
scheduling (as support), 125
security systems, 125
software, 124
technical support, 125
traditional obligations, 123
tuition funds, 125
upgrades, 125
users' fee, 125
revision, 27-29, 51, 72, 128

S

salaries, personnel, 88
scholarship, professional, 117
security records, 104-105
security systems, 125
sharing experiences/making connections, 133-140
colloquia, 135
computer-user grapevine, 135
conventions/conferences, professional, 135, 137
information sheets, 138
journals, professional, 137, 139-140
local discussions, 135
networks/networking organizations, 138-139
newsletters, 138
presentations, 135-137
publications, professional, 134, 137, 139-140
ethical/theoretical/philosophical concerns, 139
teacher networks, 138
travel costs, 139
with budget limitations, 139

workshops, regional curriculum, 135, 137
writing projects, 135
sign-up sheet, 96
slide presentation, 136
social aspect of writing, 10, 12, 27-28
software, 4, 58, 88, 104, 108, 110, 118, 124, 131
spelling checkers, 48
spreadsheet packages, 48
staff schedule chart, 99
staffing labs/classrooms, 4, 116-119, 123, 126
student-generated survey, 90-92
subdirectories, 62
supplies, cleaning, 125
supplies, expendable, 88, 124

T

teacher-generated evaluation, 92-93
teacher networks, 138
teacher training, 47-56
advanced, 55
and professional goals, 48
and professional needs, 53
as tutorial, 52
benefits of, 48-49
access to computers, 55
service credits, 55
stipends, 55
computer applications of, 55
hands-on practice, 52
in computer literacy, 52
introductory program, 53-55
obstacles to, 49-50
lack of specificity, 50-51
lack of training, 50
language barrier, 50
training sessions, 51-52
technical assistance, 42-45
technical support, 42-45, 125
see also computer specialists
technophobia, 49
tenure and promotion, 117
text-analysis programs, 48
traditional
classrooms, 29, 47, 64-65
computer labs, 8
instruction, 116
language skills, 10
literary pursuits, 117.